Break Free

A Guide to Decluttering Your Life

Dear Joseph,

Break Free to Live Free!

SAAHIL MEHTA

PASSIONPRENEUR
P U B L I S H I N G

Publishing information
Publishing, design, and production facilitated by Passionpreneur Publishing,
A division of Passionpreneur Organization Pty Ltd, ABN: 48640637529

www.PassionpreneurPublishing.com
Melbourne, VIC | Australia

To My Parents
I will always remember the sacrifices you made to ensure that my sister and I had an upbringing one could only dream of and the constant shower of love. I love you, and thank you.

To Ekta
You are the spark that reignited the leader within and were instrumental in me becoming the best version of myself. Thank you for being by my side on this incredible journey, and I love you.

To Alisha and Yuvraj
Your smiles every morning light up my day. Wanting to lead by example has made me a better person. Thank you for putting me to the test every week.

TESTIMONIALS

I had the pleasure of sitting in on a few of Saahil's talks. With each session, there were rich insights and learnings. Saahil has gone through a transformational journey that has upped his game as a professional, a husband, father, and human being. There are so many learnings in his journey that I have been able to take away and reapply. Also had the pleasure of seeing my team awed and fascinated when he offered a session at the company and it was rated one of the most engaging sessions of the year. Highly recommend listening to his journey and inviting all those around you to share in these nuggets of wisdom.

Mona Ataya, CEO Mumzworld,
Pioneer and Leader in the Vertical E-commerce Space for
All Things Mother, Baby, and Child in the Mena Region

Thanks Saahil for a great session! I'm clearly taking away some simple and useful tips to improve my physical and mental well-being. Even more helpful during times of isolation!

Vishnu Taimni, MD—Print Category,
HP Middle East, Africa and Eastern Europe

Very easy to understand and implement. Covered many aspects of decluttering. Decluttering of mind, body, and surrounding space. Overall, highly recommended.

Great job, Saahil :) and thank you for helping others to embark on their decluttering journey.

Seema Ved, Financial Controller,
BofA Securities

Saahil's book has done an awesome job of both educating and inspiring me to take action in decluttering my life. Just the clear, actionable distinction between "wants" and "needs" and the possibilities that open up are worth much more than the price of the book. There is so much more about my body, my relationships, and my mindset. Highly recommend.

Henry Chidgey, Serial Entrepreneur,
Executive Coach and Founder, Osage Consulting Group
Burnet, Texas, USA

An authentic, insightful, and impactful presentation on the topic of decluttering, by someone who is a living example of this practice. Goes well beyond the basics of getting rid of material possessions, leading each of us to self-examine how we are living our lives.

Mazen Omair, President & CEO,
Momair Trading LIC

It's an honour to have Saahil on board as part of our Safe Space Network. In order to inspire our community, we work with experts across numerous topics to deliver better ways to manage our mental well-being. The Declutter Your Mind series was positioned perfectly to help us better understand how to peel back the layers, to reveal the simplicity of life beneath.

Dani Hakim, Co-founder,
Safe Space Dubai

My good friend, Saahil Mehta, has written a must-read book, *Break Free*. In it he talks about how to declutter our lives in our family, business, community, and self. The pace of our lives has increased exponentially with significantly higher levels of stress and anxiety. Saahil offers us specific tools and choices that allow us to simplify our lives physically, materially, intellectually, and emotionally. By doing this we can become more free and effective with our lives. This enables us to perform at a higher level. I urge you to read and apply these most important principles.

Warren S. Rustand, CEO,
Summit Capital Consulting, LLC

Saahil's session on decluttering was incredibly powerful. His authentic and humble delivery of his message raised me to a new level of understanding of life's purpose and my own soul plan. I would definitely recommend it as an eye-opener for something much bigger.

Nita Maru, Solicitor and Managing Partner,
TWS Legal Consultants

I was already interested in the subject of decluttering and simplifying one's life, and Saahil's talk was the perfect opportunity to hear first-hand from someone who is currently well on that journey of how/where to begin with tangible ideas, tools, and stages for the journey. Saahil is an authentic speaker, eager to empower and inspire his audience.

Dina Yazbak, Research &
Innovation, Kaykroo

Saahil's decluttering talk changed me. Four months on, I now wake up early enough to get the most important things in my life done before most others roll out of bed. We've all read about the benefits of getting up early, but I found Saahil's story of what he's been able to achieve by actually doing it inspiring enough to make me want to change my own journey!

Ahmed Al Akber, CEO,
Hellochef.me

Saahil's story and journey is inspirational. Being reminded that it actually takes very little to have a fulfilling and enjoyable life, and that accumulating things is rarely the solution for finding inner peace, was very valuable. Getting rid of baggage as well as people and thoughts that bring you down is important. My key takeaway was the way I treat my time and how I take care of my mental well-being. I recommend this book to anyone who is looking to improve their life and ready to make some changes.

Olivia Manner, Founder,
Hellochef.me

Saahil is a rare breed, especially for our times when the draw of materialistic life is so alluring. My guru (spiritual teacher), Swami Chinmayananda, would often espouse a life of simple living with high thinking, and this is exactly what Saahil embraces and teaches by example.

His life philosophy of decluttering, which he generously shares in his coaching sessions, is not some new revelation, but indeed time-tested, ancient wisdom from so many faiths, with a twenty-first-century man's earnest application, that it rings true to all audiences. I walked away feeling inspired and grateful for the reminder of how we should all live: in the "flow" as opposed to upstream. At which point we can all experience the universe's abundance and grace.

Wishing you continued success on your voyage of self-discovery. May you attain Eternal Bliss, Saahil.

Laxmi Gulab, Aspirant

I've never thought of myself having a cluttered mind or approach. Having known Saahil for many years as a friend and entrepreneur, I really didn't know what to expect. However, within minutes into it, I found myself dissecting several events, thoughts, and items. I was "decluttering" while I was listening to him! It was extremely insightful and made me look at issues using a different approach.

Rohan Mehta, Business Development Director, Petrochem

Hearing Saahil share his journey was really eye-opening for me! With all the self-development work that many of us are doing, we tend to focus on awareness, learning, meditation, routine, etc., and we fall in and out of all the above many times. Of course, Saahil touched on all these points but always went back to decluttering. It is just a word, but the way he talked about it, he gave it so much meaning and it all made sense ... and it all falls into place with this one word if you follow it mentally and physically!

Sima Haroun, Founder & Curator, Boom & Mellow

Saahil's unmasking journey and his personal path to decluttering was astounding. He presented excellent examples of achieving an organised home, office, or car that greatly reduces stress in your life— imagine always knowing where to find your keys! He even took it a step further where the clutter not only reflects material objects but it is also actually a pile of decisions that haven't been made.

As he painted a vivid picture, it helped me grasp the true essence behind his message. That there is always a choice—that is where Saahil's dialogue hit the nail on the head. It will be those choices which will allow you to make more conscious decisions, making you feel less dispersed and more focused throughout your own journey when you give yourself time first. An inspirational session and I was glad to be a part of it.

**Vic Bageria, CEO & Chief Visionary Officer of
Xpandretail Powered by Savant Data Systems**

Saahil's book is not only generous and compelling, but the effect of his vulnerability in sharing how it feels to declutter one's physical space and mind linger on in the consciousness like ripples created in a pond after the disruption of throwing a pebble in its still water. Inspired by his drive for self-growth and compassion for life, I find myself reflecting on his ability to let go of what is not important in life to be better able to hold on to what really matters.

Rana A. Batterjee, Au.d

Saahil is a guy who is so sorted at such a young age. A guy who heard his inner voice and eventually discovered himself and his calling at the right time. Kudos to him and his belief. His journey is liberating. He must continue sharing, so more people can benefit from his liberating experience.

**Shilpa Shenoy, Director,
TOBS (The One Business System)**

Saahil, similar to Tim Ferris and Robin Sharma, is able to practise what he preaches. Saahil's holistic approach to decluttering really pushes us to delve deep into our consciousness and remove the unnecessary from our life. The book is personal and enlightening with many tips and to-do's that one can use in their daily life.

Vishal Mehta, Director,
Lumex

This truly remarkable human being took us all (at least me) on this amazing journey of "decluttering." What's purely fantastic is that Saahil has done this from the inside out. Just by hearing Saahil's journey I got such insight into the potential each of us has to continue to grow and aspire to be our best self! Keep it up, Saahil, you are an inspiration!

Sherina Jethwani, Fitness One on One

Decluttering is a word I never knew before. It was a new topic and I wasn't really excited at first. Although, after I read what Saahil had to say, I was blown away! I was easily able to relate to his examples. After reading about what led him to start decluttering, I was motivated to do the same. I learnt a lot that day, all thanks to Saahil. Every day, I try to follow Saahil's path to clear my body and soul. Thank you for a wonderful learning experience, Saahil!

Dheesh Ved, Aditya Birla World Academy,
IB Year 1

Decluttering is essential for life; however, not many of us are conscious about it. I greatly enjoyed and valued Saahil's book as he explains this concept through his personal journey. He shares the deeper meaning of decluttering, which needs to happen in all areas of life. I learnt how he decluttered—from objects, people, tasks—which is a process to clear the mind, body, and soul. The more we detach from things and people who do not elevate our purpose and soul, the more space we create for newer, purposeful things to happen in our life. In summary, my takeaway was that we need to declutter from energies that don't serve us to receive the energies that will serve us and this needs discipline and conscious living. Saahil has always inspired me to greater and deeper levels in life. I wish him a blessed journey ahead.

Meher Mirchandani, Director,
Manrre Logistics Fund

Saahil's approach to decluttering life is something everyone should utilise. Who does not want more headspace!

Moustafa Hamwi, CEO,
Passionpreneur Publishing

Eliminate what does not matter. Just focus on where you can make a positive difference and do that, and everything else, just let go. All that stuff that you don't care about anyway is clutter, just get rid of it.

Marshall Goldsmith, Thinkers 50 #1 Executive Coach &
Only Two-Time #1 Leadership Thinker in the World

TABLE OF CONTENTS

ACKNOWLEDGEMENTS

This book wouldn't have been possible if it weren't for the following people, whom I want to thank:

My family:

My parents and in-laws for my fortieth birthday gift money, which provided the finances to make this happen.

Shamina, my baby sister, who has always been one of my top supporters, and given me positive encouragement.

Vishal D., my brother and best friend, for being a sounding board throughout this journey.

My extended family who have shown me that blood is thicker than water.

The Kanchan Tara Sancheti family, for accepting me fully for who I am rather than what I am and making me feel like a son rather than a son-in-law.

My mentors:

Henry Chidgey, the biggest-hearted Texan, who always brought me back on track every time I derailed.

Warren Rustand, for putting together the state-of-mind retreat that changed my life forever.

My business partners:

The entire team at Passionpreneur for providing their tough love, guidance, and support to make this book a reality.

Gautam Ganglani from Right Selection, who showed me how to go from good to great, and enhanced my career.

Shane Mansell, my co-founder at ResNet World, who took over greater responsibilities to enable me to complete this book.

My friends:

Ala, Amit, Dharmin, Diana Pravesh, Rajesh, Sharad, and Vinayak, my personal board of directors, who were the catalysts in my transformation.

Sanjay, for sharing with James, who in turn told me not to keep the knowledge to myself and to share it with the world.

Aparna, Bilal, Deepti, Fadi, Maryam, Priyanka, Rakhee, Ruchir, and Walid, for supporting me at various points of my journey, and making this book a possibility.

Ramsey, for being my voice of reason, and always being there.

ACKNOWLEDGEMENTS xvii

Devna, Miten, and Vishal P., for the epic times together on the roller coaster of life.

My body healers:

Dr. Shefali, Dr. Gvosden, Dr. Niveen, Matt, Xhaferr, Jomon, and Rhys, for showing me how to care for my body, allowing me to go within and transform.

My communities:

Entrepreneurs' Organization (EO) for providing a safe environment, where I could be vulnerable without being judged, and transform myself into the person I was meant to be and live a life full of passion and purpose.

The Palanpuri community of Antwerp, which felt like my extended family, considering that outside my nuclear family, everyone lived elsewhere.

The Marwari gems and jewellery community in New York, for welcoming me as one of their own.

For everyone who has touched my life, I thank you, for I would not be where I am otherwise.

Most importantly, I would like to thank my life partner, my best friend, the one who has supported, tolerated, and most importantly, accepted me every step of the way on this journey of breaking free—my dearest wife, Ekta.

ABOUT THE AUTHOR

You may know who Saahil is by now, but just in case you are flipping the pages before you buy the book, then here is a quick introduction to him.

Saahil is an entrepreneur, author, and a passionate mountaineer.

Saahil has scaled four of the tallest mountains in the world—a dream he had harboured since childhood. But only once he conquered his self-limiting mindset and habits, was he able to reinvent the complete spectrum of life—from mental focus to physical excellence and from beautiful relationships to efficient environments. With a singular focus on "decluttering" what no longer serves his life's true calling and purpose, he was able to scale the actual summits of the world as well as the metaphorical summits of personal mastery.

Saahil believes that once you master the art of decluttering the non-essentials from the four dimensions of life, you truly empower yourself to *Break Free* from these illusions of limits and rise to manifest the best version of yourself. With this philosophy, he was able to scale the summits of Kilimanjaro, Elbrus, Chopicalqui, and Kala Patthar on Mount Everest in his very first attempts!

While on the one hand Saahil leads his life with absolute "ahimsa," the art of non-violence, and evangelises this virtue, when it comes to personal mastery and performance, he loves to destroy his limits and consistently conquer himself. With his debut book, *Break Free,* he shares his personal journey of how he transcended all odds to scale the summits of his dreams, and how you too can dream up new personal summits every day, once you have mastered the art of decluttering life by adopting his foolproof process of breaking free…

Go to www.saahilmehta.com for more information on how to break free to bring peace within and scale your summit faster.

Congratulations on taking the first step to decluttering your life. Just picking up this book shows how much you value yourself. You are an **amazing** human being, and I am so glad you have taken the courage to start your journey to break free.

Clutter is nothing more than shunned confrontations.

—Saahil Mehta

Do you know what these shunned confrontations do? They keep you from:

- living a healthy, stress-free life
- achieving financial abundance
- finding your true purpose and passion.

I refer to this as mental clutter, essentially a weight that is chained to your legs. How are you expected to soar to new heights if you are dragging this weight around?

Take a moment to shut your eyes and imagine what your life would look like if you got the tools to cut this chain and break free.

Pretty fantastic, right?

Before I continue, I want to highlight one misconception, which is that happiness lies in the external world. The good news is that you have all the answers. We just need to remove the clutter to see more clearly. Are you ready to overcome mental clutter and find peace within?

Once you start to remove the clutter, the results you can expect are

- more time to pursue your passion and priorities
- greater focus and awareness in all areas of life
- stronger and deeper relationships with those who matter
- high energy and clarity of purpose each day
- a life lived with love and joy rather than fear and stress.

I am just an ordinary guy who has achieved extraordinary results and found peace within. This book puts together over four years of my experiences of removing mental clutter in my life and breaking free.

> *To live is the rarest thing in the world. Most people exist, that is all.*
>
> —Oscar Wilde

My purpose in life is to spread ahimsa. I realised very quickly that peace on the outside can only be brought by bringing peace on the inside. I now share a very methodical four-step process you can apply in your life to break free from the mental and physical clutter holding you down and living a life of greatness.

This book is not just another motivational or inspirational book. This is a book that will provide you with the necessary tools that can be implemented in a logical manner to remove the clutter from your life one at a time to eventually break free and live a purposeful life.

To find peace within, some changes will be required, which could result in big shifts in your life, be it your relationship with money, people, or food. If you think you can overcome mental clutter with patchwork, you are highly mistaken. If, however, you understand that we will go to the root and resolve the clutter there, get ready to transcend and break free.

Ready to overcome mental clutter and bring peace within? Time to turn the page and commence your journey.

1

HOW DECLUTTERING HELPED
ME FIND MY PURPOSE

Who am I?

I was born pure but within moments, I was given a name, a nationality, and—when I grew a little older—a religion too. These are the labels that have been bestowed upon me, among many more, that have determined my path in life. I felt disconnected, however, as if someone kept pushing me to live the life that was expected of me, a life confined to the norms of society, my community, and my family. Coupled with that was my desire to make everyone happy, but at what cost? I wish I knew what I know now, which is that making everyone else happy is an impossible task. Not only did I set myself up for failure, but I also started to lose my true identity as I tried to become the person others wanted me to be. This put a great deal of pressure on me, which led to a high level of stress and anxiety. I felt as if each of my limbs was tied to a horse and was being pulled in different directions. The limbs represented my parents, my spouse, my kids, and my work. Where was the focus on self? The end result was that I felt trapped, whereas I wanted to break free.

I would look in the mirror but would not fully recognise myself. I would see someone of Indian descent but did not feel that way as every time I visited India I would be labelled a foreigner. I was born and brought up in Belgium, but I did not feel Belgian, as people would see me and say I was Indian. What was my true identity? Why was I looking at my physical self rather than my inner self? Even though the universe was guiding me, I did not see the signs, as I was too caught up with the noise around me. However, every now and again, I would see the signs more clearly, and my inner voice would get louder. Being a lover of mathematics and the sciences, however, I always let logic prevail and went with mind over heart, soul, inner voice, intuition, or the many other names it is called.

I do want to mention at this stage that my childhood was amazing. I lived in a beautiful town in a great environment within an amazing community and with wonderful parents. I lived in the quaint town of Wilrijk on the outskirts of Antwerp in Belgium, surrounded by beautiful greenery and lush parks and everything within bike-ride distance. The town was filled with very kind and humble residents and was so safe that milk and laundry would be left on the doorstep of the house and payments would be made every two to four weeks. My parents came from humble backgrounds where both of them had to use a shared bathroom in the building during their early years as they didn't have one in their apartments. They gave my sister and I everything they did not have, which was the best education, the latest toys, lots of clothes, and multiple holidays each year. Most importantly, we were showered with love. Even with that, I felt somewhat lost. Rather than trying to find myself I tried to fit in, which usually meant that I was doing some of the following:

- participating in activities that I did not feel comfortable in;
- trying to be like the other kids so I would be more like them; and
- avoiding confrontation by not voicing my mind.

Basically, I was doing things to make others happy regardless of how they made me feel. In fact, I used to worry so much, when on a visit to the doctor in my early teens, I was told that if I continued down this path, I would get an ulcer. One of the many warning signs that I did not take seriously enough.

Instead of addressing various issues at their core, I just allowed more and more layers of clutter to surround me, adding more masks and taking me further away from my true self.

I always used to believe I was my true self until a pivotal moment changed my perspective. In the spring of 2016, I was on a trip to the Dead Sea to celebrate the wedding of a dear friend, Fadi Fallaha. During breakfast with Maryam and Bilal, a couple from Dubai, I listened to my inner voice and opened up about the challenges I was facing from my body, which were big enough to be irritants but not bad enough to visit a doctor—at least that is what I felt at the time. This is where I got a glimpse of the power of vulnerability; I spoke about my condition in a safe environment, and they shared the condition of their family, which helped me better understand mine. They gave the contact of their doctor, and my decluttering journey began, even though I did not know it yet.

A few weeks later, I was on a trip to Spain with my forum from the Entrepreneurs' Organization—essentially what I would call my personal board of directors. We were on the magical island of Ibiza, surrounded by enchanting waters, soft grainy beaches, beautiful weather, and my kind of music, that is, house music. This was a truly liberating experience, as my default being was to impress or please others, whereas here, the environment created was one without judgement, allowing for freedom of expression of the self. This environment lasted four days and was euphoric. In fact, I was so blown away that on the way back home, I got out my diary to note down my experience and share it with my beloved wife without forgetting the details.

During this process, tears started to trickle down my face and did not stop for half an hour or so. Prior to this experience, to see me cry was extremely rare, as it showed weakness, which is not manly at all. Coupled with my poker face, I had the nickname of "Iceman." I asked myself, what on earth is going on?

I realised that I had commenced on my path to finding my purpose. Through awareness, I understood that I became vulnerable by removing my masks and becoming my authentic, true self. I was able to find a deeper connection with my being and in turn find my true state of happiness.

I could not recall the last time I had felt this way for several days. How long had I been hiding behind these masks? How many masks was I wearing? By looking to make everyone else happy, I had found only emptiness and unhappiness instead. Although the world we live in is full of judgement, I knew that if I could feel even half of what I felt during my trip, I would already be in a much better place than I was. I started to look at what clutter was weighing me down and began to untether myself from it, and thus my journey of decluttering began.

I got a call from the doctor and went back in anticipation of my results. It was shocking, to say the least. The doctor was surprised that I was not lethargic and believed I was running on adrenaline! I found out that I was dangerously lacking in two major vitamins (B12 and D3) and I was highly intolerant to dairy, almonds, and eggs. Mind you, I have been a vegetarian all my life, and in fact, I even used to make fun of vegans (due to my love for dairy) and say, "Thank God, I am not vegan, otherwise I would have to shoot myself." It is ironic that this should happen to me. Within days I started to see the following benefits, which were a result of eliminating foods that were harming me and supplementing my diet with the essential vitamins I was lacking:

1. The irritation in the back of my throat after most meals disappeared. It always felt as if something was stuck, which resulted in my trying to cough it out.
2. I no longer woke up with a blocked nose.
3. The release of flatus reduced heavily.
4. I no longer had energy dips during the day.

In the following five months, having lost 10% of my total body weight, which was primarily fat, the next step of decluttering became easy, as most of my clothes did not fit me anymore. As my size had remained pretty constant for two decades, I had accumulated a lot of clothing and hence had much to give away. As I started giving away my material items, something very interesting happened to me—I felt lighter and free. Each item I owned occupied some real estate in the physical world as well as in my conscious or subconscious mind. The worst part was that several items had no functional value nor did they bring joy in my life, so essentially they were occupying space in my mind rent-free! With each item I gave away, not only did it bring happiness to another being, but I now had space to fill with whatever mattered most to me—more time with the family, doing things I love, enriching my mind, and so on.

Using the same framework, I continued down this path to declutter people and my mind. Decluttering people is not about getting rid of toxic people, but rather being neutral around them so that they do not affect you negatively anymore. In addition, decluttering people is about removing the clutter in the relationships that matter most. I now spend more time with people that raise my energy levels. Strangely enough, the stronger my energy levels became, the more I attracted amazing people in my life.

Decluttering the mind was the hardest for me. To look in the mirror and have conversations with myself was both nerve-racking and liberating at the same time. Initially, I couldn't even look into my own eyes as I could not recognise what I had become. In pleasing others, I had lost my own identity and was completely disconnected. When I finally built up the courage to focus on myself, I would procrastinate and the fear would put me back in my comfort zone. However, with the momentum I had picked up from the constant benefits of decluttering other areas of my life, I realised it was time to engage with myself and let the mind's journey begin. I covered several areas, including acceptance, assumptions, freedom, and emotions, with the hardest being forgiveness. It was so easy in the past to avoid these conversations or blame situations. In my avoidance of confrontation, however, confrontation with the self was the one that should not have been dismissed. The more I decluttered, the more liberated I felt, which gave me the momentum to continue on this path. Now this does not mean I will never buy something I want or I will never lose my temper; however, both have drastically reduced due to awareness of the self.

The journey of decluttering allowed me to remove the noise in my life, which has resulted in

- more time to pursue my passion and priorities
- greater focus and awareness in all areas of life
- stronger and deeper relationships with those who matter
- high energy and clarity of purpose each day
- living my life with love and joy rather than fear and stress.

What is most amazing is that this process of decluttering has improved not only my personal life but also my family life, my business, and my connection to the community. I never expected the results to be so huge over the last four years, and I cannot wait to see what will come in the journey ahead. All I knew along the way was that with each removal of clutter, I felt clearer and more liberated. Best of all, the beauty of this process is that it is accessible to everyone, as it does not cost any money!

Initially, several people thought this was a passing fad or made fun of my various changes in lifestyle. Over time, however, when my so-called fads became rituals, those around me slowly started to accept me for who I am. For those who did not, decluttering people just got a whole lot easier. It was certainly hard at first, as those nearest and dearest to me were not able to keep up with the pace of change I was going through. The greatest challenge was with my wife, Ekta, where we started to drift apart. I was changing at such a rapid pace that she could not keep up and did not recognise me. I cannot even fathom the confusion in her mind as I was evolving into someone very different from the man she had married. I kept asking myself, should I stop? Should I slow down? Although we faced several challenges, I knew deep inside that all the changes were pure and I would have to endure some pain for a stronger future.

I used to be obsessed about finding my purpose of being or my "why." If anything, this caused more anxiety, until I came across an interesting thought that concluded, "The purpose of my life," to put it simply, "would be to leave my soul in a better place than when it entered my body." When I did find my specific purpose, however, it happened when I least expected it. The answer was always there—I just did not see it. Through a sequence of events, it became clear that my purpose is the path of ahimsa. I am the spark that brings peace within and around.

I wanted to carry on with this purpose of mine and create an impact to use the purpose for a greater good. One big question I had was: "How can I create an impact?" I am just one person. It all changed when dining in a restaurant where I was given a card with the following message:

It takes one to change a few, a few to change many, and many to change the world. It all starts with one.

I now know my purpose in life is to spread this message so that I can help people struggling with mental overload to scale their summit faster through a four-step decluttering process to break free and find peace within. This book focuses on removing physical and mental clutter and my objective is to reach audiences worldwide with my methodology to help them on their journey of liberation to become their authentic self and live a life of purpose. Over 90% of illnesses and diseases today are based on lifestyle and stress, NOT genetics. This has given a huge boost to the health and wellness industry, which is making people aware that the journey required is not on the outside but rather inward. We were all born pure. My goal is to get you back to that pure state through the art of decluttering. Why? A pure individual will love over hate, hug over fight, live in harmony with life rather than destroy. This ultimately means a more caring society which leads to a more blissful world.

I have not studied decluttering, so why am I to be considered an expert? While completing my bachelor's and master's degrees in electrical and electronics engineering at the University College, London, one thing became quite apparent: the results from our experiments were always different from what we had learnt in theory due to various variables. What I am sharing with you in this book is what I have experienced in the four-plus years I have been on this journey, which has given me results I could never have imagined: my body is no longer in pain, as I stopped the activities that were causing harm; my marriage is at an all-time high, as I made my wife my no. 2 priority (after myself, of course); my businesses are prospering with my minimal involvement, as with focus I am now working on the business rather than in the business; and I have accepted myself and now know I am plenty and more. This has allowed me to focus on my purpose (which also happens to be my passion). The best part is, there is so much more to come. I love what

I do, I am good at it, the world needs it, and I am getting paid for it (bonus).

> *My message is my life.*
>
> —Mahatma Gandhi

Decluttering is not a process but a journey that is only possible through awareness. The next chapter is going to talk about how you can become more aware of your actions and thoughts, which will make your journey far more impactful towards self-discovery and living a liberated life.

Question: What labels have been put on you, by yourself and others?

_____

_____

_____

_____

_____

_____

_____

_____

EXERCISE: Complete the wheel of life and give yourself a ranking out of ten for each section.

1. Rank your level of satisfaction with each life area.

2. Connect the dots to create a new perimeter.

3. Which area do you want to focus on the most?

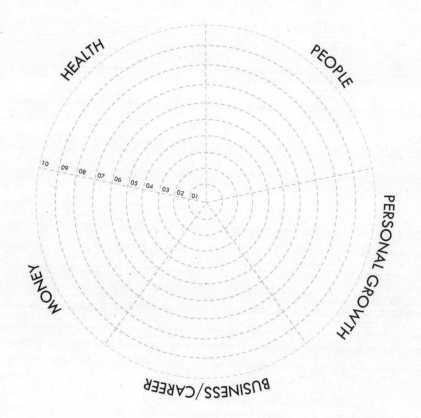

2

WHO/WHAT IS YOUR NO. 1 PRIORITY?

Change your perspective and all becomes clear.

The first step in crafting the life you want is to get rid of everything you don't.

—Joshua Becker

We often talk about what is to be added in our life to progress, but often forget about what is to be removed, which is preventing us from making progress.

In this chapter, you will learn the four stages of decluttering in order to liberate yourself and become the person you were meant to be and achieve greatness. The four stages to live more authentically and with greater purpose are as below:

1. Decluttering the mind.
2. Decluttering the body.

3. Decluttering people.
4. Decluttering the material world.

Now, I am not saying you are not authentic or have clutter or live without purpose. I am simply saying we all have clutter that is holding us down and preventing us from reaching our full potential. I humbly request you continue to read with an open mind, as we can all agree that we do not know what we do not know.

Before we continue any further, I want to share a story that will highlight my point. Growing up in Antwerp, Belgium, a treat I absolutely loved was ice cream. The three flavors available at the supermarket were usually vanilla, strawberry, and chocolate. If we were lucky, we got an ice-cream sandwich that consisted of both vanilla and chocolate. I thought this was my world and what an amazing world it was. It all changed one day when Häagen-Dazs opened up in the city centre. I still remember walking into the beautifully lit store, with sensational aromas making me salivate with anticipation over the fifteen-plus flavours of ice cream beautifully displayed, and trying sample after sample before locking in on pralines and cream. Once I became aware of this new world I never knew existed, I came to the realisation that I must forever remain a sponge, ready to absorb the beauty out there.

My objective is for you to change your perspective and see things from different angles.

By the time you finish reading this, you will have the essential framework to start removing clutter from your life to overcome mental overload.

When I make this much money, I will be happy.
When I get that promotion, I will be happy.
When I find a partner, I will be happy.
When I buy that item, I will be happy.
When I get that many followers, I will be happy.

Do the above sound familiar? In each case, it is a condition or circumstance that you have set for yourself in order to be happy. Why is it that we need to depend on external items to be happy? What if I told you that the physiological state of a human is to be happy? The choice is yours to be happy and content regardless of the external world.

We are looking in the wrong direction.

I want to highlight three misconceptions in our lives today:

1. Happiness lies in the external world.
2. There is not enough time in the day.
3. Spending time with self is hard.

Family will come and go, friends will come and go, wealth will come and go; however, time is really our most valuable asset, one that we will never get back. Keeping that in mind, how much time are you spending on yourself, reflecting? The distractions have become so many that at every opportunity, a large proportion of people reach for their mobile device even when going to the bathroom! I am sure once the devices are waterproof, they will enter our showers too. You spend the most amount of time with yourself. Now is the time to improve that relationship. Why be the second-rate version of someone else when you can be the best version of yourself?

Previously, when I had alone time, I would jump to my phone in order to make sure I was using time efficiently as being with my thoughts felt as if time was being wasted. I was very reactive and felt like the hamster on the wheel, running but not always clear about my direction. Today my perspective has changed, and I long for alone time on a daily basis to reflect which, ironically, has freed up time. How, you may ask. One word—focus. This has enabled me to be more proactive and have a better grip on my day.

All the answers lie within. While at a seven-day Vipassana (silence retreat)—where all forms of communication were ceased and I spent a lot of time with my favorite person, me—I came to the conclusion that when all distractions are removed, the answers become clear. It was so apparent that I concluded that moving forward, any important decision would be made after detaching myself from everything and being alone in nature until the decision became clear. In one case, specifically regarding a case of betrayal, my decisions evolved from violence, where pain was imminent to all those involved, to a more compassionate approach where unity became a possibility, which is much more in line with my core values.

This can only be achieved through a heightened state of awareness. The *Oxford Dictionary* defines awareness as *"knowledge or perception of a situation or fact."*

To better understand this concept, let me share the difference between awareness and unawareness. In the mind of a layman, there are two perspectives:

The first is the doer.
The second is the one on whom the action has taken place.

If you carefully examine your actions, you will notice that you are not always in control. If someone says something hurtful, you lose your temper; if someone is flirting with your spouse, you get jealous; if someone holds you tight, you fall in love. You immediately react with these feelings without there being an interval between the event and the reaction. Depending on which button is being pressed, you react differently, so my question to you is, who is in control? Everybody likes to be in control or think they are in control, but in a state of unawareness, which is described above, control very much is in the hands of the doer, as they trigger your emotions.

To become aware is to add one more step to the above:

The third is to be the observer.

Here you are creating an interval between the event and the reaction, where you are observing the event and seeing what is happening within. As you have consciously distanced yourself from the event and are purely acting as a witness, not the enjoyer, this is the moment of awareness. During this moment of consciousness, of complete awareness, you have the ability to decide how you wish to react. This is your decision and not one that is being controlled by anyone else. Your reaction is being made with full awareness.

Let me demonstrate with an example of unawareness versus awareness. My best friend goes off on me, accusing me of insulting him in front of our friends. The unaware version of me would react with anger and defend my position, leading to an unpleasant outcome. The aware version of me would take a moment to observe what is happening to my best friend and understand that it is not like him to react in this manner. Consciously, with compassion and love, I would ask him, "Is everything OK with you? I can understand the words may have hurt you. However, it is not like you to behave in this manner, and as your best friend, I am concerned there is something deeper bothering you." (Mind you, there can also be other scenarios.)

During the observation I may have noticed that he needed to vent and I would just remain in silence, allowing him to do so as I realise he may not have any other avenue at that moment in time.

As most of the world lives in unawareness, being aware may seem strange. Imagine someone yelling at you and through awareness you do not react, as that was the conscious decision you had made. You are no longer under the control of another where you react based on the button they press. People may feel they are losing control over you and may even think of you as abnormal, but the truth of the matter is that you have broken free from the bondage of others. Welcome to awareness.

It is time to focus on the self. When you have clutter in your life, whether physical or mental, it is basically like a ball and chain attached to your leg.

The more of these you have, the greater is the weight holding you down and preventing you from soaring. How do you think this affects your energy levels? We cannot deny our body is made up of trillions of cells with each cell consisting of energy, which can be either negative or positive based on your state of being. If you now change perspective and look at someone as an energy field rather than the physical body, you will be able to feel their presence from a distance. To better understand, you can see a bonfire from a distance; however, you can also feel the heat (basically a form of energy) from a distance. Using the same thought process, you will be able to feel the energy of a person from a distance.

> *Energy is contagious, positive and negative alike. I will forever*
> *be mindful of what and who I am allowing into my space.*

> —Alexe Elle

Now, if you are in a negative state of being, what type of energy do you think you are radiating? Negative, of course! That will do one of two things: (1) repel people/things that are in a positive state, or (2) attract people/things that are in a negative state. So if we start to focus on the self through awareness we will be able to identify the various balls and chains (the clutter) holding us down and start to address them one at a time by cutting loose and working towards a clutter-free life, allowing us to reach new heights and results we never imagined. This will move us towards a positive state, which would attract people/things that are in a positive state and repel (or convert if the energy is really strong) people/things that are in a negative state.

It is time to make yourself the no. 1 priority. You spend so much time with yourself; imagine how much more amazing life can be if you improve that relationship with the self. So the question that you must ask yourself is: What do you want to attract in your life?

I want to attract _____

_____

The next question you have to ask yourself is, what is your self-worth? To answer this question, I want to share a story:

A boy asked his father, "What is my worth?" To answer the question, the father gave a stone to his son and told him to go to the market to sell the stone on the condition that he could only show two fingers when asked the price. At the market, a lady loved the stone and felt it would look great in her garden, so when she asked the price, the boy showed two fingers to which she replied, "$20 is very fair." He ran back to the house and shared his experience, after which the father told his son to visit the curator at a nearby museum. The curator was intrigued with the rarity of the stone and wanted to add it to the collection. When he asked the price, the boy simply showed two fingers to which the curator was glad to offer $2,000. Shocked at the difference, the boy once again ran back to his house to share the experience with his father. Next, the father sent his son to a precious-stone dealer who, after investigating the stone, was overwhelmed to see such a rare stone and offered $200,000 when the boy showed two fingers. The son almost collapsed in surprise and went running home in a confused state, wondering how three people had offered three different amounts for the same stone. The father sat his son down and told him, *"My child, you have already discovered the answer to your own question. The greatest value of your life is just like this stone: In the market, you are worth*

$20. In the museum, you are worth $2,000. But if you place yourself with the precious-stone dealer, you're worth $200,000! The value of your life is exactly where you place yourself."

How do you find your self-worth? Start by asking yourself these questions:

> If you do not love yourself, how do you expect others to love you?

> If you do not have faith in yourself, how do you expect others to have faith in you?

> If you do not trust yourself, how do you expect others to trust you?

Remember, out of the tens of millions of sperm that were swimming upstream towards the fallopian tube with a mission to fertilise an egg, only a few hundred made it close to the egg due to the natural barriers in a woman's body. Out of that, just one made it, and the miracle that is you happened. Imagine the odds of you even being born! You are an amazing human being, and I am so glad you have the courage to start to declutter your life.

> *If you get the man right (or the woman, of course), you get the world right.*

> —Matthew Kelly

This is why I do what I do—provide tools to declutter your life and remove the weight that you have been holding on for so long, which allows you to go back to your authentic self, a beautiful soul filled with compassion and love. If the world goes back to this state, there would be no hatred, no wars, no crime, and we would all look at each other as beautiful souls and live in harmony with each other and Mother Earth. Just imagine everyone with the heart of a four to six-year-old child.

The beauty about everything I have shared till now and will continue to share in the rest of this book is that everyone has the ability to go within. It does not cost you any money, only time, and by now you should know that you are your no. 1 priority. What are you waiting for?

I have heard all sorts of excuses as to why not now. My answer is simple, like the story of Sir Roger Bannister. On May 6, 1954, Bannister not only broke the record for the mile run which was held by Gender Hagg of Sweden, but he also broke the four-minute barrier which people thought was impossible for this distance. In addition, doctors and scientists said that attempting to do so was also dangerous to one's health!

They did not know it was impossible so they did it.

—Unknown

What fascinates me the most about this story is that the record only stood for forty-six days, after which it was broken by John Landy. The only change was in the mindset, which changed from "it is impossible" to "it is possible." Pause here and think about all the times where what blocks you from achieving greatness is you . . .

- I can't run that distance
- I am unable to wake up early
- They will probably say no if I ask them out on a date
- I will not succeed

With all the negativity we throw at ourselves, we fail to realise that it keeps building up, churning inside of us, resulting in mental health challenges which is becoming the new global pandemic. What makes it worse is that we are comfortable discussing physical health issues, but mental health seems to remain a taboo for many. This is further amplified, as people tend to keep this inside, leading to all sorts of issues.

To understand the state of how severe this has become, let me share some facts from the World Health Organization (WHO) (https://www.who.int/news-room/facts-in-pictures/detail/mental-health):

1. Around one in five (20%) of the world's children and adolescents have a mental disorder.
2. Depression is one of the leading causes of disability, affecting 264 million people (that is, one in thirty people worldwide).
3. About half of mental disorders begin before the age of fourteen.
4. Almost 800,000 people die by suicide every year; one person dies from suicide every forty seconds. Suicide is the second leading cause of death in individuals aged fifteen to twenty-nine years.
5. People with severe mental disorders die ten to twenty years earlier than the general population.
6. The global economy loses about US$ 1 trillion per year in productivity due to depression and anxiety.

I have come up with a simple methodology to start your journey to liberation and work towards finding your purpose. As you can see, the diagram below looks like an archery target, where as you get close to the bullseye, the process goes inwards to outwards. For that very reason, we'll start with decluttering the mind and then we will move to decluttering the body, people, and the material world, ultimately helping you break free and find peace within. By tackling the easier items first (low-hanging fruit, as they say), the positive results will give you the drive and momentum to tackle the more challenging items.

Declutter the Mind

Here, you will learn how to stop letting your mind get in the way of reaching greatness. We will discover how to:

- Start each day on a high and with more energy
- Understand why there is no reason to worry
- Identify your no. 2 priority
- Forgive your past

Declutter the Body

Here, you will learn different techniques to allow your body to work optimally for you, allowing you to go deeper within. The topics covered are:

- Monitoring essential vitamins and minerals
- Getting better sleep
- Hacks on healing your body

Declutter People

Here, you will get the tools to create stronger and deeper relationships as well as be yourself even with people who have caused much pain. Here we will be exploring:

- Loving people for who they are rather than what they are
- Understanding that everyone is on their own journey
- Not letting people drain your energy levels

Declutter Material Things

Here, you will understand how to reduce items you own with the objective of identifying what really matters. You will learn:

- The key differences between want and need
- Detachment from material objects
- Creating space for new possibilities

Break Free

As you progress on this decluttering journey, you will learn to live a more authentic and purposeful life, achieving results beyond your imagination. Here, your core values will also become crystal clear.

Now that you have reached the end of the chapter, let me highlight the misconceptions one more time:

1. Happiness lies in the external world.
2. There is not enough time in the day.
3. Spending time with self is hard.

Now you know happiness lies within you.

Now you know there is ample time when you are focused.

Now you know that you are your no. 1 priority.

Before you proceed, however, I want you to ask yourself how badly you want to be free, as freedom does not mean you just do what you want; rather, it is the strength of character to do what is noble, right, good, and true. Freedom means to be the best version of yourself rather than being a second-rate version of someone else. To get to this state, however, courage, humility, and discipline are required. Certain activities may have to be sacrificed, and certain people may need to be sacrificed; so I ask you one more time, how badly do you want this?

EXERCISE: With this sense of awareness, make a list of all the things (physical and mental) that weigh you down. Just pick up a pen and a piece of paper and write from the heart. Keep adding to this list as and when you think of something.

....

....

....

....

....

....

....

....

....

....

....

....

....

....

....

....

....

....

....

....

....

....

....

....

....

....

....

If you are ready to:

- Spend more time to pursue your passion and priorities
- Have greater focus and awareness in all areas of life
- Pursue stronger and deeper relationships with those who matter
- Start each day high on energy and clear on purpose
- Live your life with love and joy rather than fear and stress, and

… break free to find peace within, I invite you to move to the next chapter. I now welcome you to turn the page to enter your mind.

3

TODAY IS GOING TO BE THE BEST DAY EVER!

Declutter the mind

The first hour of the morning is the rudder of the day.

—Henry Ward Beecher

How you start your day is essential to how effective your day will be. Start each day being high on energy for maximum impact. If that is not enough, your positive state of being will also result in you radiating energy at a frequency that will attract more positivity in your life. Read on if you want more positivity in your life.

> *I want to take this moment to congratulate you on starting your decluttering journey—it will be one of the best decisions you have taken. I am so excited for you and cannot wait to hear your results.*

This chapter will cover four of the five significant changes I made in my life that have allowed me to break free from the shackles I put on myself. The fifth significant change, which is forgiveness, will be covered in the next chapter.

Morning routine. Take control of your day and go through a routine to energise yourself. How you start your day can impact the rest of the day.

My no. 2 priority. Do you feel you are being pulled in different directions? Could this be because your priority keeps jumping between work, family, and community? Learn how to make this process simple. You may recall from Chapter 2 that you are your no. 1 priority, hence we are focusing on your no. 2 priority here.

Why worry? I met a man once who told me I had no reason to worry. At first, I thought he was crazy, but the more I listened and reflected, I understood he was absolutely right. I will be sharing this simple concept with you later in the chapter.

Acceptance. How often do you doubt yourself? How often do you wish you were taller, smarter, thinner, better looking, stronger, or so on? Is your self-worth based on the validation of others? Allow me to show you another perspective that helped me to love myself again.

What does your typical day look like? Mine used to feel like a rat race, where my typical day looked like this:

1. Wake up at 6:15 a.m. to get the kids up and rush them to get ready.

2. Ensure they eat breakfast and leave at 7:10 a.m. for the school drop.
3. Workout at 8:00 a.m.
4. Breakfast at 9:20 a.m.
5. Get to work at 10:00 a.m.
6. Work, which was mostly reactive and with a task list that kept growing.
7. Home by 6:30 p.m. to have dinner with the kids.
8. Spend time with the kids and put them to bed by 8:00 p.m.
9. Spend time with wife/parents/friends.
10. At some point, get to bed.

Where was me time? Although I would get it in spurts here and there, was that enough to improve the self? As discussed in Chapter 2, the no. 1 priority should be me; however, it certainly did not feel that way.

Although time was progressing, I really did not feel I was moving forward. It almost felt as if no matter how hard I tried, even though the businesses were moving in the right direction, I had too much mental clutter and felt I was living a reactive life rather than a proactive one. In a nutshell, I did not have control over my life.

What made matters worse is I had no clue what I wanted in life. A dear family friend once asked me, "Where do you see yourself at the age of sixty?" And I was blank. I want to be successful but what does success mean? I want to be rich but what does rich mean? I want to have amazing relationships, but what does amazing mean? I want to be healthy but what does healthy mean? It was clear that I had no direction but just a general "I want to be rich, successful, healthy, and have great relationships" attitude, which did not really amount to anything.

I want to share with you this scene from the book *Alice's Adventures in Wonderland* by Lewis Caroll:

Alice: Would you tell me, please, which way I ought to go from here?
The Cheshire Cat: That depends a good deal on where you want to get to.
Alice: I don't much care where.
The Cheshire Cat: Then it doesn't much matter which way you go.
Alice: So long as I get somewhere.
The Cheshire Cat: Oh, you're sure to do that, if only you walk long enough.

It was time to get control over my life again. I had to start removing the clutter that was fogging my view.

I would like to start by sharing a very powerful affirmation that I write daily.

"I have the power to change my life for the better. To get it right and get the desired results."

This is a reminder that it is I who is responsible for myself. "You are a master of your destiny, not a victim of your history," as my dear friend and mentor Moustafa Hamwi would say.

Our mind is also exceptionally powerful. So powerful that it can be your best friend but also your worst enemy. Let me share the story of the two wolves to highlight this point.

An old Cherokee is teaching his grandson about life. "A fight is going on inside me," he said to the boy. "It is a terrible fight and it is between two wolves. One is evil—he is anger, envy, sorrow, regret, greed, arrogance, self-pity, guilt, resentment, inferiority, lies, false pride, superiority, and ego."

He continued, "The other is good—he is joy, peace, love, hope, serenity, humility, kindness, benevolence, empathy, generosity, truth, compassion, and faith. The same fight is going on inside you—and inside every other person, too."

The grandson thought about it for a minute and then asked his grandfather, "Which wolf will win?"

The old Cherokee simply replied, "The one you feed."

Let me now share how we can focus on starving the evil wolf and feeding the good wolf.

MORNING ROUTINE

After spending a week in Idaho at a life-changing State of Mind retreat with Warren Rustand, whom I also consider a mentor, I realised the importance of implementing a morning routine to energise myself and break free from my typical reactive day. Before I get into the routine, however, I want to highlight three conditions that must be followed for maximum impact:

1. No snoozing. Do you really want snoozing to be the first action of the day that sets a precedent for the remainder of the day?

2. No digital devices (phone/tablet/computer/TV) or newspaper. Imagine reading/seeing something you do not like that puts you into a negative state of being. I do not know about you, but it can take me several hours, if not the whole day, to get back in a good state. Do you want to risk starting your day in a negative state of being?

3. Ensure you are able to conduct your morning routine without any distractions. In my case, once the kids wake up and are full of positivity, they want to spend time with me and so I am unable to do my routine. I work around that by waking up one hour earlier.

Let me now start with the morning routine. Please note, this is what works for me and should be used as a starting point. Feel free to make amendments as you see fit, but make sure you have a routine.

1. **Movement (15 min).** You have hopefully been sleeping for seven to eight hours, where your heart rate had decreased by 20%–30% (just enough to keep your vital organs functioning and not taking more than required for healing). To get the heart rate back up, do any form of movement you enjoy, be it walking, star jumps, or the sun salutation. Just move.

2. **Breath work (10 min).** Take deep belly breaths. Put your hand on your belly and feel the belly moving in and out as you take deep breaths (several people breathe from the chest). This is important to get oxygen to all your cells to come alive.

3. **Meditation (20 min).** There are many forms of meditation that you can try and see which one feels right for you. Meditation is important to create a balance between the mind and heart. Remember, when you went from a crawl

to a walk, you did not give up after falling the first time. Practise to get into the rhythm, and if it does not work just sit in silence and reflect.

4. **Journaling (15 min)**. I have noticed that writing has a great impact on thought. I write the following in my journal every morning:
   a. Three things I am grateful for at that moment.
   b. Three things I am excited about at that moment.
   c. A positive affirmation that I select from a few that I have put together.
   d. Asking for and giving forgiveness to everyone to cleanse myself.
   e. I end with writing, "Today is going to be the best day ever!" thanks to my children who got it from *SpongeBob SquarePants*.

As you can imagine, I am now full of energy and ready to take on the day. Now, if you throw anything at me, it may knock me down a little but it certainly will not knock me out.

MY NO. 2 PRIORITY

Thanks to Warren Rustand, I also became crystal clear about my no. 2 priority. Prior to this, as expressed earlier in the chapter, I would be conflicted between work, family, and community (which includes friends), and would often fluctuate between the three. Now, of course, there are times when one area of your life will require greater attention; however, I am speaking about the overall priority here. I personally chose family because work will come and go and so will friends. And even within family, there are parents, spouse, and kids. So I ended up choosing my wife as my no. 2 priority. If life takes its toll, my parents will pass before me and the children will eventually move out. All that will be left will be my wife and I certainly do not want to wait until then to ensure our relationship is as best as it can be. I love her deeply and have made a conscious decision that divorce or remarrying is not an option. The moral here is to be clear on what your no. 2 priority is, so that when you come to a crossroads between two options, there is no confusion about which path to take.

WHY WORRY?

In 2019, I came across this concept, that there is absolutely no reason to worry. Now you may think I am nuts when I say this but look at the next figure and see for yourself that there really is no reason to worry.

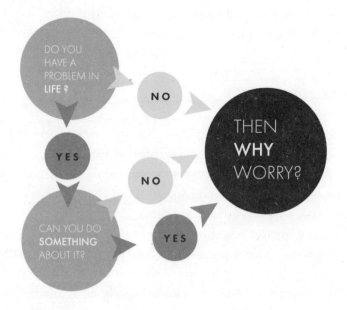

Let me take you through the process. Do you have a problem in life? If you answer no, then there's no reason to worry. If you answer yes, the next question is, can you do something about it? If you cannot, then why on earth are you worrying? No matter what you do, you have no control over the outcome, so stop worrying. If you can do something about it, then go ahead and do something about it, and then there is no reason to worry. So you see, whatever the situation may be, there is no reason to worry.

You may say that your problem is more complex, to which my answer would be, break it down into parts where you can do something about it and where you cannot. That already reduces the worry until you put in motion the steps to resolve the things you can control. Sounds too good to be true? Go ahead and do it and see for yourself how effective it is.

This also includes the future, as we tend to fear something that has not happened because of our assumptions and worry about it in the present.

ACCEPTANCE

If you do not love yourself, how do you expect others to love you? If you do not believe in yourself, how do you expect others to believe in you? If you do not accept yourself, how do you expect others to accept you? How about standing in front of the mirror and saying, "I am plenty and more"? Does that mean you do not want to improve anything and just want to accept yourself unconditionally? Yes and no. If you need to build strength for your next adventure or learn a new skill set for your work, go ahead and do it, as that is working towards a goal you require. Following the same methodology of the "why worry" concept, put the wheels in motion rather than judging yourself for not having the ability.

I want to share a story about Bruce Lee, one of the most recognised individuals in the world of martial arts. Did you know that his left leg was almost one inch shorter than his right? Rather than giving up on his dreams, he accepted his limitation and worked with it to become an international legend.

How many times have you wished parts of your physical body were bigger/smaller/etc.?

How much time and money are you spending on products to make you look younger?

How much are you going to continue to blame others for your shortcomings?

No one judges you more than you judge yourself. Develop patience and avoid becoming your own worst enemy. Accept yourself for everything you are and you are not. Stand in front of the mirror and say, "I love you. I believe in you. I am plenty and more."

Statistics from the World Health Organization (WHO)

1. Twenty percent of the world's children and adolescent population have a mental disorder.
2. Depression is one of the leading causes of disability affecting one in thirty people worldwide.
3. About half of mental disorders begin before the age of fourteen.

4. Suicide is the second leading cause of death in individuals aged fifteen to twenty-nine.
5. People with severe mental disorders die ten to twenty years earlier than the general population.

I want to share three short stories about when I did not accept myself and the effect they had on me.

Chasing the six-pack

I would look at myself in the mirror and dream of having a six-pack. There is nothing wrong in having dreams. However, in this case, I was chasing vanity so that I could impress others when taking the shirt off. I did not stop with the abs, however; it was also my arms, shoulders, legs, etc. to chase the perfect body (whatever that is!). Thinking back, I laugh as I realise how little my physical appearance matters to me today. With my love for adventure and the mountains, I now focus my workouts towards any activity that will make it easier for me physically during these adventure trips. If I end up getting a better-looking body in the process, I just consider that a bonus. For those who are wondering if I have a six-pack today, the answer is no. ☺

Doing what it takes to look younger

Over the years, the grey hairs on my head have been increasing, from a few to today's salt-and-pepper look. Even though I look at age as just a number, I still fell into the trap of colouring my hair to look younger, which I believed would make me look and feel better. Over a period of six months, I partially coloured my hair (I say partially because we only targeted half the hair to make it look natural).

Apart from wasting time and money on vanity, I was also applying chemicals on my head, which is harmful to both the environment and me. After the third time, I reflected deeply on this and saw myself as a hypocrite, as I was pushing others to accept themselves when I was not even accepting myself. It was from that day onwards, I accepted not only myself but everyone around me. A few months later, when I decided to stop using any form of hair gel, I told the barber to give me an army cut (level 1 on the sides and level 2 on top). I was about to embark on a spiritual journey and wanted to remove this distraction to go deeper within. I have stopped using any hair dye and hair products with chemicals.

It is because of . . . that I am not happy

Every time I encountered a shortcoming in my life, I would quickly blame anything or anyone over myself. I was clearly not ready to accept that the error could have been mine. At work, if we did not get the results expected, I would be quick to blame it on the industry or salespeople. At home, I would not feel fulfilled and would blame it on my spouse or parents. I then came across the following positive affirmation that opened my eyes to a perspective I had never considered:

> *I have the power to change my life for the better. To get it right and get the desired results.*

I am responsible for my life and no one else. I immediately stopped blaming people or situations. I accepted where I was and decided where I wanted to go and made the necessary changes in my life to get there.

It is imperative that you spend time alone to reflect on your life. Remove your distractions and understand that if you do not invest in yourself, you cannot expect to get the results you desire. You will find many things that will question your beliefs, your core values, and what you have learnt till now. It is time to unlearn what you know and relearn what you will find out. The more time you spend with yourself without any distractions, the deeper you will be able to go.

My most profound thoughts have risen from spending hours alone surrounded by nature. When I was distracted, I used to speak a lot and understand little. I now speak less and listen to observe and understand everything around me, and most importantly, understand myself.

You now have the tools to start each and every day with maximum energy for maximum impact by implementing a morning routine that consists of movement, breath work, meditation, and journaling. Make sure you are not snoozing or picking up your phone the first thing in the morning. In addition, you are aware that there is no need to worry, and no matter how complex the situation, you are able to split it into two categories: one where you cannot do anything about and the other where you can do something and take necessary action to remove the worries, allowing you to be more focused.

You are now clear about the direction in which you want to proceed by choosing your no. 2 priority, preventing you being pulled in all directions. Whether you choose your spouse, family, community, or work, be crystal clear, as fluctuating between them can cause a great deal of anxiety and stress.

Most importantly, you have learnt to accept yourself for everything that you are and see an amazing person, who is not defined by just physical appearance but by the purity inside.

EXERCISE

In order to start decluttering the mind, identify which day this week you will start your morning routine by getting up before everyone else.

Day of the week to start:

Start putting post-it notes on your mirror, cupboard, desk, etc., with the words "I am plenty and more." Keep reminding yourself to accept you and be the best version of yourself rather than a second-rate version of somebody else. Write COMPLETED in the space below once you have done the exercise.

Make a list of all the items that are making you worry and start splitting them into two lists: one where you can do something about it and the other where you cannot. Stop worrying about things where you cannot do anything, since worrying will not change the outcome, and put a plan of action for those items where you can control the outcome.

Worry item	Do something about it	Cannot do anything about it	Plan of action

Stop worrying about these after putting a plan of action together

Stop worrying about these immediately!

Now it is time to tackle what I consider two of the biggest obstacles when it comes to the mind—ego and forgiveness.

4

FORGIVENESS

Time does not heal, only suppresses

To forgive is to set a prisoner free and discover that the prisoner was you.

—Lewis B. Smedes

How long is the pain from your past going to hold you from achieving greatness? Until you forgive and break free, you are choosing to carry the pain of the incident with you wherever you go.

By the end of this chapter, you will learn the tools to forgive so that you break free from the pain and create a new way to remember the past. Whether it was the person who cut you off on the road or the betrayal of a member from your inner circle, they will no longer cause any pain in your life and if anything, you will even learn to thank them for helping you evolve.

Forgiveness goes hand in hand with ego. How many times have you said, "I can never forgive him/her"? It is the ego that does not allow you to forgive. The bigger the ego, the stronger the resistance to forgive.

The most important point to keep in mind as you read this chapter is this is not about the other, but rather this is about you. I only care about your progress and will share what you can do to come out stronger.

Before I continue, I want to share what forgiveness is not:

1. Forgiveness is not condoning the offence.
2. Forgiveness is not ignoring or forgetting the offence.
3. Forgiveness is not reconciliation.
4. Forgiveness is not removing the consequences.

Now that we are clear on what it is not, let me share an incident. I have been betrayed several times in my life; however, it was only when the betrayal was from a member of my tribe did it cut deep, as it was least expected. The first incident that had a significant impact was back in 2007, where a third-generation friend decided to sell his stake in a real estate investment to us, while hiding the fact that the project was over budget and way behind schedule (which came out in the courts during litigation). My error in judgement was to accept an e-mail reply on the same without doing a detailed due diligence, as I never expected a friend to mislead me this way.

I was told that time heals, but I can tell you with 100% certainty that is absolutely false. Time just suppresses. I would hear his name and the painful memory would trigger. I would hear a song on the radio from our time together and would relive the moment. Although I was not thinking about it all the time, the pain would surface through various triggers as described. How could I get this out of my head? How could I move forward? I had no idea how he was living his life, but I did know that the negativity was still churning inside me. Here is a different perspective—I was causing this pain to myself by holding on to it rather than letting go through forgiveness.

Before I continue, I want to highlight that I still trust people that I come across, but now I constantly validate, a great lesson taught by a mentor I admire very much, Henry Chidgey, based out of Texas in the United States.

In September 2018, I was meditating in my hotel room in Hong Kong. With my core value being non-violence, it became apparent that I had to forgive in order to stop hurting myself. As I reflected on all the areas that required forgiveness, two other incidents came to my mind, where I had hurt others and wanted to ask for forgiveness as well as forgive myself for my actions. I pulled out a paper and pen and started to write my letters of forgiveness, starting with the ones where I wanted to be forgiven, as I found that to be an easier starting point. After completing the letters, I typed them up on e-mail and sent them to all three.

This was a purely a selfish act where I wanted to release the negativity inside me without expecting any response. As soon as I clicked on 'send' I felt a huge weight being pulled off my shoulders. I had finally set myself free from the pain I had held on to for a decade.

Are you ready to liberate yourself?

I will now share with you the four stages of forgiveness that I have applied in my life that have helped me remove the heavy clutter holding me back all these years:

1. You have been forgiven.
2. Forgive as you have been forgiven.
3. Forgive yourself.
4. Prevent forgiveness.

Before I start, however, I want to share with you what the process of forgiveness is not:

1. Forgiveness does not need to be communicated. This is a process within you and informing the offender is optional.
2. Forgiveness does not condone what the person did. You are simply breaking free from the negative bond and no longer giving them any importance in your life.
3. Forgiveness is not pretending it did not happen or that you were not hurt. It is an acceptance of the occurrence and seeing it as a gift.

Now let's get back to the four stages.

1. You Have Been Forgiven

Although forgiveness seems hard at first, think about all the times in your life until now when people have forgiven you. If you are like me and have screwed up several times in this journey called life, the list will be very long. Is it your parent who had to deal with your troubles in school? Is it your spouse who dealt with your frustrations as you unleashed them? Is it the business colleague you let down because you did not meet the project deadline? Whatever the case may be, look back and acknowledge each time you were forgiven. If you have been forgiven so many times, don't you think it is time you start to forgive too?

2. Forgive As You Have Been Forgiven

As mentioned earlier in the chapter, without forgiveness, the negativity will keep building up inside you each time the memory surfaces. This negativity causes chemical imbalances in your body, which can eventually become chronic illnesses. From a purely selfish perspective, why do you want to cause harm to yourself? Now that you have acknowledged that it makes sense to forgive, let me share four methods that have been most effective for me:

1. Write a letter of forgiveness. With each word you write, the negativity is being transferred from within through the writing instrument on to the paper. As you already know, energy cannot be created or destroyed, and can only be transferred. Don't think and just let the words flow out. This is not for anyone to read and no one will judge the letter. Once you have completed the process, safely burn the letter. Let it go and all the emotions with it to make space in your life. Think of a word that represents what you want to bring into your life, such as love, peace, joy, etc. Sit with it and savour the moment.

2. Rather than asking yourself, why is this happening to me, ask yourself, what is this teaching me? Once you change your perspective from a negative to a positive outcome

by focusing on the lesson learnt, it helps relieve the pain. Although the occurrences felt awful at the time, when you look back now, these instances shaped you to become who you are today—an amazing human being focusing on decluttering their life to achieve greatness.

3. Understand the intentions of the other person. In several instances from my past, I realised that the intention of the other person was pure; however, the outcome turned out to create animosity. Take time to be clear on the intentions, which could have been from a place of compassion and love but unfortunately resulted in friction.

4. Get inspiration from others who have forgiven in situations far worse than yours. One day, as I was having great trouble with forgiveness, I heard of a mother who forgave the killer of her son. I could not believe this so went on Google to search "mother forgives her son's killer" and was surprised to see how many such instances were out there. Her words sent a chill through my bones: "The only way I was able to live on and be present for my surviving son was to forgive him." If a mother can forgive her son's murderer, then I can certainly forgive too.

3. Forgive Yourself

We are often too harsh on ourselves, even when the person we offended has forgiven us. You have two choices really: continue to batter yourself down or forgive and become free. To forgive yourself also means you need to be honest and take responsibility for your actions rather than making excuses. Go deep within to understand why you did what you did. During this exploration, you may find a deeper issue that needs to be resolved. In either case, this healing process will allow for a stronger you to emerge. The methods shared in the previous section can be applied here to forgive oneself. You cannot love yourself fully until you forgive yourself.

4. Prevent Forgiveness

Once you start to master forgiveness, the next step is not to get hurt in the first place. You cannot control the actions taken by others, but you can control your own. Whatever the reason may be for the other person to perform their actions, you can choose to not let it affect you. You just focus on being a good human being and enjoy this beautiful life for everything it is.

What if the person you want to forgive is someone you see frequently—a family member, colleague, or someone in your circle of friends? After the writing of the letters, I felt free and had a good grip on how to forgive. That is when life decided to throw me a curveball, which I will now share with you.

You know that gut feeling you get when you are certain something is not right, but when the person involved is someone near and dear, your mind tells you it simply cannot be. In addition, whenever I presented things that alluded to outcomes I considered odd, I was told that I was being paranoid and this made me doubt myself, as the people involved in this story are individuals with core values I thought were similar to mine.

It turns out that my gut feeling was right and I was faced with another betrayal, but this time, we would be seeing each other often because of work. Just my luck.

This is where I learnt a valuable lesson about giving enough time to reflect in order to heal. The challenge of meeting the offender often is that your emotions get triggered, which delays the process of forgiveness. I had to distance myself and spend more time with myself, uninterrupted, in order to reflect deep within. I would practise, daily, during my morning routine, where I would go through a cleansing process. I would write, "I forgive all living beings in the universe. May all living beings forgive me. I do not have any animosity towards others, and I have friendship towards all." In addition, I would constantly be checking in with myself and be more aware of my feelings. Thanks to applying all the methods I have shared till now, I was able to forgive in less than twelve months . . . certainly a lot faster than my previous episode of one decade.

Forgiveness to me means that the triggers that result in hatred disappear. "How can you forgive?" you may ask. "You should take revenge!" I am not going to lie; in all my experiences of betrayal I have thought about revenge, especially when high on emotion. Although it may feel good temporarily, it would still not resolve the conflict within, which was what was required to bring me peace. I had to remove my ego in order to reduce the resistance to forgive. I am not going to allocate any energy towards the offenders anymore as they no longer have a place in my life. I wish them the best in their journey moving forward, and perhaps one day we will be more than two people who know one another.

Forgiveness is directly correlated to the strength of your ego. The bigger the ego, the harder it is to forgive. Let us better understand the meaning of the word, ego. In Latin, the literal meaning is "I." A definition I recently came across, which is an acronym, is Exaggerated Glorification of Oneself.

With most people, identity is linked to position, possessions, or achievements. What happens when you lose any one, if not all three? Does that really change who you are?

- Position brings responsibility
- Possessions are to bring comfort
- Your self-worth is not defined by your achievements

If you really want to know who you are, focus on the part of you that never changes. Ego has been completely removed, as you are no longer defining yourself based on your position, possessions, or achievements.

Here is a short story to highlight the benefit of removing your ego. A bird was flying with some food in its mouth and noticed a flock of birds following behind. The bird thought they were following in admiration and became proud. After a few minutes, the bird realised the others were only interested in the food. At that moment of realisation, the bird dropped the food and watched all the other birds dive to get it. Once the bird let go of its ego, the sky became its own.

You are not forgiving for the other person; you are forgiving for yourself. When the pain caused by the offender in the past continues to affect you today and follows you into the future, you have two choices: continue to hold on to the pain or let it go. When you choose to hold on to the pain, resentment, and anger, you are being harmed far more than the offender, which can also lead to various illnesses. Forgiveness sets you free, allowing you to enjoy the present and the greater things in life.

If you need that extra boost to start your process of forgiveness, recall all the times you have been forgiven. Gradually, work towards not getting hurt at all. Why would you want to give that power to someone else?

You are your biggest critique, so don't be so hard on yourself and certainly don't let that ego get in the way. Life is too short to keep holding on to that bitterness in your heart.

As a bonus, you can even inspire others to take similar action and be the catalyst to improve the lives of others.

EXERCISE

Set a date for when you want to write your letters of forgiveness, either to yourself or to others. Remember this is an exercise for you only, so let the words flow out as no one is there to judge. Once you have transferred the negativity from your body on to the paper, safely burn the paper and watch it go to ashes. As you remove the negativity, be clear about what you want to bring into your life and reflect on that. Make sure you are in a safe space during this exercise to allow for any emotions that may arise as a result. Do not hold back and let it flow.

Date to write letters of forgiveness:

We can now start to focus on the body and ensure our body does not become a distraction. A body working more optimally results in greater success.

5

IF IT DOES NOT FEEL RIGHT, IT PROBABLY IS NOT

Declutter the body

Let me describe a typical day in my life, before I began focusing on the self. I would wake up each morning with a stuffed nose, feel bloated throughout the day (particularly after meals), get an irritation in my throat after most meals, and feel lethargic at various points of the day, which led to a near-death experience. Little did I know this was because of what I was eating. What if I told you that all these feelings disappeared and I got my life back after changing my diet and adding mineral and vitamin supplements?

By the end of this chapter, you will be able to have a better understanding of your body through a three-step process.

1. Eliminate food items that are causing harm.
2. Get the right nutrients to fuel your body.
3. Eliminate harmful substances from your skincare products.

If it does not feel right, it probably is not.

—Saahil Mehta

Based on my experience, it is crucial that you are aware of how your body feels and not to take it lightly if it does not feel good, especially if it is a chronic condition. Although I was aware of the bloating and the energy dips throughout the day, I did nothing about them, as they didn't seem big enough to consult a doctor. In addition, during various routine blood tests and a full medical at a leading hospital back in 2013, I was told everything was fine; hence I just accepted these symptoms as something I would have to live with. Little did I know that I was dangerously low on Vitamins B12 and D3, which almost cost me my life and that of my spouse.

Looking back, the warning signs were there, but I guess no one really noticed and I just thought it was due to a lack of sleep or pushing myself hard. I have fallen asleep at the table in restaurants, on the sofa while chatting to friends, in nightclubs, and on the phone with my then fiancée. Being in a long-distance relationship across the Atlantic, I had mentioned to her that I would probably fall asleep while talking and that she should not take it personally, as it was not her, but me. Even with all the warnings, every time it happened, I got an earful. ☺

I was driving home one evening with Ekta next to me, who was fast asleep. I must have completed 80% of the distance with another five minutes to go before reaching home. Suddenly, as if the movie stopped abruptly, the curtains closed and I fell asleep behind the wheel. I woke up seconds later, hearing loud screaming and feeling the violent movement of the car as it rode over large rocks before it came to an eventual stop. With my heart in my throat, all I could think about was Ekta, my parents, and how young we were to die. Each and every airbag inflated, except mine. I looked over to my right and I could see Ekta in tears but OK, there was no blood visible and she seemed to be conscious. We both got out of the car, and it was only then I realised how bad the crash really was. The car was completely crushed from all sides and one tyre even flew off! We were lucky to walk out with only minor bruising. We were lucky that there was no other car or civilian involved in the crash. We were lucky that someone with a big heart came to check up on us and bring us home. A decade later, the vision of that crash is still in my mind . . . not accompanied by fear but as a reminder that I must live to the fullest, as I do not know if tomorrow will come. Back then, however, I had still not woken up.

You are not what you eat, but rather what you absorb.

—Saahil Mehta

Our body, simply put, is an amazing and complex machine. Treat it well and it will work well for you. If you treat it badly, however, knowingly or unknowingly, challenges will start to surface. Although I would be a little naughty and eat higher amounts of sugary items or indulge in fried foods high in salt every now and again, overall, I was eating what one would consider a healthy, balanced diet.

Unknowingly, however, I was hurting my body each and every day causing the machine to malfunction in certain areas. I did not know at the time but I was constantly bloated, releasing gas in both directions fairly often (embarrassing in many cases) and would also have to visit the bathroom more than I would have liked. I often woke up with a stuffed nose, which also meant I would be breathing more from the mouth, resulting in a dry throat, which came with its own set of irritations (especially after meals). I also used to break out a lot on my forehead as well as the back of my arms. I had accepted these symptoms as just being a part of me.

We have all heard the phrase "you are what you eat." I later found out from an integrative functional doctor that in fact you are not what you eat, but rather what you absorb. Even though my wife and I were eating the same food, the blood tests we both did would highlight that only I had severe food intolerances and dangerously low levels of certain vitamins. The difference was that she was absorbing the vitamins and minerals far better than me, because of a much healthier gut.

What is food intolerance? Food intolerance occurs when you have difficulty digesting a particular food. Common symptoms include intestinal gas, abdominal pain, or diarrhoea. Please note, however, food intolerance can be mistaken for food allergies, which trigger the immune system, whereas food intolerance does not. To the best of my knowledge, in the medical field it is not clear whether food intolerances cause a leaky gut or vice versa.

Whatever the case may be, the challenges in my gut were caused by my mental state. Until I had a safe space to talk about the challenges I was facing in my life and the effects they were having on me, they were all being internalised rather than being let go.

Although I addressed this in more detail in Chapter 3, what I can tell you at this stage is that the brain has a direct effect on the stomach and intestines. For example, the thought of eating can release the stomach's juices before food gets there.

So, what is a leaky gut? It is essentially increased intestinal permeability where the tight walls of the intestinal wall loosen, allowing for harmful substances such as bacteria, toxins, and undigested food to pass into your bloodstream. The symptoms as per *Medical News Today* (https://www.medicalnewstoday. com/articles/326117#symptoms) are shown below and I have highlighted in **bold** the symptoms I had:

- chronic diarrhoea, constipation, or bloating
- nutritional deficiencies
- fatigue
- headaches
- confusion
- difficulty concentrating
- skin problems, such as acne rashes, or eczema
- **joint pain**
- widespread inflammation

Whether you have a leaky gut or not, the following are great techniques you can apply to ensure you eat better so that your body does not become a distraction.

1. If you are eating any packaged food, start reading the ingredients and ask yourself if you are happy consuming those items. Once I started looking, I was shocked to see how much sugar there was in items that were positioned

to be healthy, AND many items even had ingredients that I just could not recognise (basically synthetic). In an ideal scenario, find a replacement if the following are listed:

a.   High-fructose corn syrup
b.   Artificial sweeteners
c.   Artificial colours
d.   Sodium nitrites and nitrates
e.   Monosodium glutamate (MSG)
f.   High levels of sugar

2. Replace simple carbohydrates (processed) such as desserts/sugared cereals/sugary drinks/refined bread with complex carbohydrates (natural) such as wholegrain breads/bran cereals/vegetables/fruits.

3. No distractions during meals such as TV/phones/reading, etc., or having to rush your meal. Distractions have shown to lead to overeating as per the Harvard Medical School (https://www.health.harvard.edu/blog/distracted-eating-may-add-to-weight-gain-201303296037#:~:text=These%20studies%20point%20to%20two,to%20eating%20less%20later%20on.). Slowing down and savouring your food can help you control your intake. Studies have shown that it takes twenty minutes after you start eating for your brain to start sending out "I'm full" messages. How long does it take to eat your meals?

4. Chew your food to break it down into smaller pieces. Digestion starts in the mouth, where the saliva produced helps break down the food (not only in the mouth but in the stomach too). This process also helps you to extract the maximum nutrients from the food you eat.

5. Diets have a very high failure rate in the long term. The key here is to determine the direction you wish to take and change your lifestyle accordingly. If you find it hard to give

something up, focus on what amazing foods you want to add that are in line with the lifestyle you want.

6. Fat has got a bad rapport over the last few decades, and I just want to clear up a HUGE misconception. Fat is required AND fat is good. The key here is knowing which fat you are consuming, as you need to ensure you are eating polyunsaturated and monounsaturated fats (found mainly in fish, vegetables, nuts, and seeds) and eliminating artificial trans fat (prominently found in highly processed foods). When it comes to saturated fats (found mainly in whole-fat milk, red meat, cheese, and coconut oil), it is all about moderation.

The last thing I want to focus on is our largest organ, which makes up approximately 16% of our overall body mass—the skin. Since it is porous, it absorbs whatever you put on it. So when it comes to living a healthy and natural lifestyle, what you put on your body is as important as what you put into your body.

Are you paying attention to the ingredients of the skin-care products you use? If you are like how I was and just buy products based on the packaging and labels, you probably do not. I decided to stop all skin-care products (including but not limited to soap, shampoo, conditioner, lotion, and lip balm) containing anything that was not natural. Just like with food, I started to pay close attention to labels and realised that most mainstream body-care products contain a cocktail of carcinogenic chemicals, allergens, and irritants which, once absorbed, make their way to your blood and lymphatic system. Why would I want that?

With the rise of e-commerce, it is so easy to now find natural skin-care products that do not have toxic chemicals, preservatives, and fragrances that are harmful to our bodies. Petroleum derivatives, preservatives, synthetic fragrances, and dyes go by many names. A few examples of common ingredients to steer clear of are cocamidopropyl betaine, olefin sulphonate, sodium lauroyl sarcosinate, potassium cocoyl glutamate, sulphates, parabens, and phenoxyethanol.

Although I was eating right (at least that is what I believed) and was working out multiple times a week, I just couldn't lose body fat, which was in the range of 24%. I had reduced my sugar intake and fried foods, stopped soda, and consumed less salt, but it just did not seem to help. In fact, it led to all sorts of challenges in my body, which I have described earlier in this chapter.

It all changed while having breakfast by the Dead Sea in Jordan, where I opened up to how I was feeling with my friends, who were fellow members of the Entrepreneurs' Organization (EO). As we follow a core value of confidentiality, I felt comfortable talking about what I would otherwise have kept to myself. Thinking that I was the only one struggling with these symptoms, I quickly realised I was not alone. My friends shared their own personal experiences and even suggested an integrative functional doctor to consult once I was back in Dubai.

After completing a blood test and an intolerance test, apart from finding out about my low vitamin levels, I found out that I was also highly intolerant to dairy, eggs, and almonds. These were items I was consuming every single day! Being a vegetarian up until then, I used to make fun of vegans and say, "Thank God I am not vegan, otherwise I would kill myself" . . . the irony!

Although I LOVED dairy, I was OK to give it up for a year in order to get the body to operate at an optimum level. My saving grace was knowing that after my body healed, I would be able to introduce dairy back into my diet. I was also told that whether I ate a small piece of cheese or the entire slab, the effect on my body would be the same, so if I wanted to "cheat" I should max out. I totally took advantage of that, and every now and again (usually when one of my favorite meals was being served), I would max out for the entire day only to feel the effects of it later in the day or the day after. A little over a year later, however, when my purpose in life became crystal clear , I chose to live a vegan lifestyle and gave up dairy and eggs forever.

My closest friends would often ask how I gave up dairy and could not believe it was true. Previously, not only did I live to eat (now I eat to live), I used to have dairy in pretty much every single meal I ate. My response to them would be, "You cannot put a price on how good I feel." Now that I have a taste of how amazing it feels when the body is operating at optimum or near-optimum levels, I never want to go back. Let me explain what I experienced.

Over a span of six months, I lost 10% of my body weight. Luckily, I had been measuring my body composition so had a baseline to compare to. Basically, my body fat went down from 24% to 13%, so a majority of my weight loss was a reduction in fat. When I stopped the foods that were harming me, my body started operating like an optimal machine, resulting in minimal bloating, better sleep (no more blocked nose in the morning), and a very high metabolic rate. In addition, my vitamin B12 shot up from 197 (recommended range is 187–883) to 807 and my vitamin D3 went up from 11 (recommended range is 30–100) to 58. After supplementing the vitamins I was lacking, my hair loss greatly reduced and I no longer felt lethargic during the day, which basically meant no more episodes of suddenly falling asleep.

For this to work, first and foremost you have to be clear about your direction. Once you are clear about this, it becomes a lot easier to make the necessary decisions that are in line with where you want to go. If you want to have a body working at optimum levels that essentially allows you to feel great and beyond, you have to start becoming more conscious of what you are consuming and be more aware of how you feel.

1. If you feel bloated or uneasy or have any other negative symptom, reflect on what you just ate. Are you seeing a repeat pattern with certain food types?
2. Temporarily eliminate foods that cause food sensitivities and see how that feels. Common items usually include dairy, gluten, eggs, nuts, soy, and shellfish. You can even get a food intolerance test done, which will give you a lot more detail. A typical response I hear is, what if I have to stop eating something I love, to which I answer, what is more important—a food item that you love or feeling great?
3. Make it achievable and easier on the mind. If it is hard to eliminate something, change your lens and just start eating more of what does not cause you any harm.

You are not what you eat but rather what you absorb. To ensure you absorb at optimal levels, you can follow the guidelines below:

1. Eat more of what you are lacking. Make sure you are getting a good balance of carbohydrates (complex ideally), proteins, and fat. Many of us suffer from starvation of nutrients and not calories.

2. Avoid processed foods, sugars, and foods that are not natural.
3. Engage in mindful eating. Chew your food to make it easier for your digestive system to absorb and enjoy savoring the multitude of tastes.

The above requires you to invest a little time to be more aware of what is entering your body. In addition, find replacements for harmful products that you are applying on your skin too.

Remember, if it does not feel right, it probably is not. Do not take a chronic issue lightly as I had done, which almost cost me my life.

Everything in this chapter can only be achieved through increased knowledge. So, first and foremost, I would suggest to get a blood test done to check your essential vitamins and minerals. As you may be a layman like me and not a qualified doctor, it would be a great idea to meet with an integrative functional doctor to better understand the results and take the necessary actions.

Increased knowledge also means to start reading and researching the ingredients of all the products you ingest as well as those you apply on your skin to ensure you are feeding the body with the right fuel to work towards optimal health.

EXERCISE

Get a blood test done to check essential vitamins and minerals. Ideally, get it checked by an integrative functional doctor.

Start reading the ingredients of all products that you are ingesting or applying on your skin and check for better options. Make a list of ingredients you were shocked to see:

Food item	Shocking ingredient

Now that we have covered what we are ingesting and applying on our body, I invite you to read the next chapter, where I will address healing and recovery with a focus on removing injuries, fasting, and how to get a great night's sleep.

6

LET YOUR BODY HEAL

Steps to optimal recovery

No matter how hard the past, you can always begin again.

—Buddha

Majority of illnesses today are a result of lifestyle. However, the good news is no matter what we have had to deal with, we can begin again and allow the body to heal. This amazing body we have is a natural healing machine. Take the necessary steps to allow the body to heal at its optimum level.

In this chapter, we will focus on three areas that I have implemented to heal the body:

1. No more injuries
2. Fasting
3. Sleeping

No more injuries. By changing your workout and/or your lifestyle habits, you can gain the benefits of avoiding injuries that essentially consume energy and time, which otherwise would be used towards healing.

Fasting. I was under the impression that I must eat three meals and snack in between to ensure I am fuelling my body due to my active lifestyle. Little did I know how much my energy levels and body efficiency would increase with the introduction of fasting.

Sleeping. Sleep was usually sacrificed for most things, unfortunately. What if I told you that it is one of the most effective things you can do for both your brain and your body? This is the time where most of your mental and physical recovery happens.

> Do you want to increase your immunity?
> Do you want greater focus and awareness?
> Do you want more time to fill with your passion and priorities?

If you answered yes to any of the questions above, it is time to start being more aware of the body as the body is always giving you signals, especially when things go wrong.

Imagine a world where you no longer have any sick days or injuries, where your body is constantly healing for optimal health. In the previous chapter, you looked at the things affecting your digestion and absorption, to prevent harming your body. In this chapter, we will focus on external factors that will enhance your healing and recovery process.

There are trillions of cells in the human body constantly trying to reach equilibrium by keeping us at or bringing us back to a natural balance. When we abuse our body, however, these cells get damaged or destroyed, sometimes in large quantities; it takes up more energy to either heal or replace these cells. *In my case, I was partaking in activities that resulted in frequent visits to the physiotherapist.*

Apart from feeling horrible when unwell or when you lack sleep, think about the ripple effects

- Your mood is off, which affects your relationship with people
- Your productivity is lower, affecting productivity in the workplace
- You are spending more time and money on hospitals/ doctors

Is that really how you want your life to be?

I will be sharing with you the three most effective measures I have taken that have led to results I did not know were possible. My immunity has reached new heights. Just to put things in perspective, the last time I was somewhat ill was in 2018, when I was coughing for about five days.

As mentioned in the previous chapter, you cannot put a price on how good you feel when your body is no longer a distraction for you to excel. Continue reading and see how to reach optimal health.

Our bodies are natural healing machines. The best example is when we have a small cut whereby our body takes different actions in order to close the wound after which the healing commences. To ensure we heal, however, the first step is to stop harming the body. In my case, I was too aggressive in my workouts, which led to periodic injuries.

NO MORE INJURIES

Between my long-distance running and heavy workouts, I spent a lot of money and time with two different physiotherapists (just to complicate matters). Having made myself my no. 1 priority, I decided that I was going to do what it took to get to the root cause of my injuries, as this was not the life I wanted to live. Rather than listening to my body, I just decided to continue down the path of pain I was on until two separate incidents occurred, which I would like to share.

The first was when my physiotherapist asked me if I was competing in sports to which I said no. His follow-up statement was, is it worth it? He saw that I was coming regularly and questioned how important it was for me to deadlift 100kg versus 70kg, for example. That was a wake-up call for me, as I quickly realised it was not important at all, apart from fuelling my ego. Effective immediately, I replaced two of my heavier workouts with yoga. What followed was amazing. Not only did my injuries come to a halt, but my body also opened up, allowing for better flow. It almost felt like there were too many blockages due to the tightness in my body.

The second was when my other physiotherapist noticed a significant difference in the size of my quadriceps. Although most of us have a muscle imbalance, this was significantly larger for me. The question was, why? After a visit to my chiropractor, I was told to get an X-ray, CT scan, and neurological test to get to the source of the issue. To my surprise, the problem was nerve-related and the good news was that it was benign. Basically, my nerves were not firing properly into my right quadriceps, which led to a weaker muscle. As a result, I immediately stopped any activity that resulted in my quadriceps getting overtired, which was primarily my long-distance running and any workout that put too much continuous pressure on my right leg. My biggest learning here was that by taking care of this one issue, several other pains in the body disappeared. As my right quadriceps were getting tired before the left, other muscles and tendons on the right side would start to compensate, causing pain anywhere from my foot all the way up to my shoulder. Earlier I used to think these were all independent aches, but I quickly realised that they were all linked.

As the regular injuries disappeared, the number of cells damaged or destroyed reduced and more energy was available for healing.

FASTING

Once I started to look at the body through the lens of healing for optimal health, my view on meals changed completely. Previously, I would follow whatever best practices were shared with me, such as

- Eat breakfast like a king, lunch like a prince, and dinner like a pauper
- Don't eat too much during meals and eat smaller meals

As with most messages I was hearing, they didn't really match and often conflicted each other. The result was I ate well for breakfast and lunch with a lighter dinner. I would, however, have snacks in between. As we have already concluded, our bodies are healing machines and this process requires energy. Once we eat, a process of digestion takes place, which also requires energy. After some basic research, I concluded that anywhere from 10% to 30% of your energy is consumed daily to digest food. The harder the food is to break down, such as proteins, the higher side of the range you would be. So my "aha" moment was that if I remove the digestion process, more energy would go into healing. After further research, I came across the concept of autophagy, which literally means self-eating. As per my research, "autophagy" is the natural, regulated mechanism of the cell that removes unnecessary or dysfunctional components. It allows the orderly degradation and recycling of cellular components. In essence, this healing process cleans out damaged cells.

As per the experts, the autophagy process initiates in humans after eighteen to twenty hours of fasting. Based on this information, I do a twenty-four-hour to thirty-six-hour water fast twice a month based on the lunar cycle. Please note you can do it as and when convenient for you depending on your schedule and healing required.

I also want to take this opportunity to share my perspective on when and how often to eat. As highlighted already, our body is our best messenger, so start listening. I now only eat when my body asks for food. Previously I ate three meals a day with a possible snack or two because that is what I was taught. The problem I faced was that on several occasions, I started to eat again even though gastric emptying was still in process (that is basically the digestion process that takes place in the stomach before it moves to the small intestine), which usually lasts from two to five hours. So basically, I was not giving my stomach a break except while I was sleeping, and so I concluded I needed to give my body a break and only eat when my body said so.

SLEEPING

While you sleep, your body produces increased white blood cells that attack viruses and bacteria that otherwise would hinder the healing process. Your immune system relies on sleep to be able to fight harmful substances. Now that we have acknowledged the importance of sleep, let me share with you the hacks I follow to ensure I get a great night's rest:

1. Eat around three hours before you go to bed. As mentioned above, gastric emptying takes between two and five hours, which means it will either be completed or close to completion by bedtime, allowing for more energy towards healing. Ideally it would be better to avoid/reduce foods that are harder to break down such as proteins or raw food.

2. Avoid caffeine after lunch. Since caffeine has a half-life of four to six hours, by the time you go to bed (assuming you had the coffee with lunch), the impact on your sleep would be 25% or less.

3. Stop using digital devices at least one hour prior to going to bed (I work towards stopping them post dinner) as they emit significant amounts of blue light. So what, you may ask? Blue light tricks the brain into thinking it is still daylight, and hence the production of melatonin, which is responsible for making you sleepy, is reduced. If you simply cannot do this every day, one solution is to purchase blue light filter glasses, which basically have an orange tint that blocks out the blue light. You can even start reducing the lighting around your accommodation.

4. Charge your digital devices outside your bedroom. There is no concrete evidence I have found to support this; however, having electromagnetic waves so close to my head just does not feel right. Even if the impact is close to nothing, at least these devices, which were distracting in my case, do not interfere with my sleep in any way.

5. Incorporate a sleep routine. The body loves routine, so whether it is some combination of brushing your teeth, closing the lights, changing into your pajamas, etc., follow the same routine so the body is aware it is about to go to sleep.

6. Sleep by around 22:00 as until 02:00 the body engages in physical recovery whereas after that until around 06:00, the body engages in mental recovery. That is why if you sleep too late, even if you get seven to eight hours of sleep, the body would still feel tired.

7. Go through a process of forgiveness to cleanse out the negativity rather than carrying that baggage with you to bed. A great example is if you have an argument with a loved one and decide to go to bed without clearing it up.

Now that you have the tools to enhance your recovery, let the healing begin.

Even though our bodies are not exactly symmetrical, for most, this does not pose to be an issue. And I want to emphasise once more, the body always sends signals when things go wrong. But in my case, I was not listening.

For years I ran long distance, which I define as distances of 10km and beyond. I completed my first marathon in London in 2002. Although my target was under four hours, which meant I had to run 10.5km/h, I ended up completing the distance of 42km in four hours and forty-one minutes which was at an average speed of approximately 9km/h. Although I was fine until the halfway mark, which I completed in one hour and fifty-two minutes, somewhere around the 35km mark, things started to go horribly wrong. I started feeling pain in my right leg as if someone was punching me on my quadriceps with each step. I had to slow down and even walk at certain points. Back then, I thought this was what runners referred to as "hitting the wall" and at that point my mind took over, as I was clear that I would crawl across the finish line if I had to, as failure was not an option. Perhaps not the wisest choice, but as an adamant twenty-two-year-old, what else could I say?!

To backtrack a bit, I had only decided to run the marathon a few months before and was lucky enough to get a spot through a local charity. I basically ran as my clothes had started to get tight and I needed a way to get back in shape. I trained very hard in a short period of time, which meant that I pulled the tendons in my feet just weeks prior to the marathon. While conducting physiotherapy sessions, my therapist told me to rest my feet to which I responded, "Can I still go skiing?" Since the foot doesn't move in the ski boot, he said it is fine if I really wanted to do that. Not the wisest decision, especially since the marathon was my priority but again, I was an adamant twenty-two-year-old. After skiing for a week, I returned to London to be told that it was OK to run, but if the pain returned, I should stop. Luckily for me the pain was in my quadriceps and not the feet, so I was able to cross the finish line.

Fast forward to 2016 and to a wiser self, when I found out about my muscle imbalance, I immediately stopped long-distance running, as it was harming my body. Rather than trying to go against the tide, I changed my workout routine to focus on what worked for my body so that I was not spending energy on healing injuries that could be easily be avoided and could focus on healing for optimal health.

For this to succeed, you have to be clear about your direction, allowing all decisions to become easier. I had decided that I would not stop until I had the answers. A lot of patience was required, as I reached several dead ends. I did not give up, however, as I was my no. 1 priority.

Once I was clear that I wanted to treat my body like a temple and increase my immunity, I also understood that my decision would mean that I may no longer be able to participate in activities I liked and would have to explore new worlds that were better suited to me. I gave up long-distance running for high-intensity workouts using body weight to ensure I still got my cardiovascular exercise. I am not saying you should give up what you love, but until your body is capable of performing that activity again, you will need to find a replacement to ensure you do not harm your body and slow down the healing process.

This can also affect your social life. Based on what kind of fasting you initiate and the increased focus on sleep, late dinners or parties will start to become less frequent. This is even more challenging if you suffer from the fear of missing out (FOMO). It all comes back to the same point of direction that I mentioned in the previous paragraphs. In my case, my optimal health was more important than anything that allowed me to enjoy life to its fullest, so I just became more selective where I said "yes."

When it comes to fasting, do not starve yourself to the point that it ends up causing more harm than good. Take baby steps and gradually build up to the stage when you do not consume anything but water.

Enjoy the journey! I have said it before and I will say it again, there is no price you can put on feeling great.

In summary, the objective of this chapter is to focus on the external factors that can impact your healing process so that your health is at an optimal level, resulting in high immunity, and your body is no longer a distraction to reach your summit.

1. Eliminate activities that are harming your body and be clear about your direction so you can pick activities that are in line with your goals.
2. Practise fasting so that damaged cells can be cleaned out and more of the body's energy goes towards regenerating newer, healthier cells.
3. Get enough sleep and ensure you sleep at the right times for physical and mental recovery.

By following tips from the previous chapter and this one, you now have the tools in order to live a healthy life with greater focus and awareness in all areas of life, and more time to pursue your passion and priorities.

If you wish to take one more step forward to declutter your body, let me share a very insightful principle from Nidhi Pandya, an Ayurvedic practitioner based in New York in the United States.

We regularly talk about imbalance but do we really know what balance is? Balance is reaching a state of homoeostatis, which in biology, is the state of steady internal, physical, and chemical conditions. This is the condition of optimal functioning for the self and includes many variables, such as body temperature and fluid balance, being kept within certain preset limits. The question now becomes, how do we reach that state? As human beings, we are warm and moist, and examples include but are not limited to our blood, mother's milk, and urine. Good flora and fauna exist in warm and moist conditions. Gratitude and compassion are warm and moist. The key words here are **warm** and **moist**.

If we look at our consumption, warm relates to hot food as well as good spices (the ones that will not burn your tongue). Moist is picking the right ingredients where even if the ingredients are dry, that can change with the addition of well-sourced oils. Something to think about for your next meal.

My next learning from Nidhi was an eye-opener and is something I practise every day. Being a diurnal species, our internal clock is in sync with the sun (also known as the circadian rhythm). Keeping that in mind and the elements of nature, given below is a perspective on how to remain in sync:

> Morning, where the dominant element is water, is cool, dewy, and sluggish. Signs of this in our body are congestion in the nose, white coating on the tongue, and a stiff body. Get your joints moving to open up and eat a warm breakfast to prevent the digestive system and enzymes shutting down.

> Midday, where the dominant element is fire, is when the sun is above and the digestive system is operating at its peak. This is when you can have your biggest meal of the day. As the sun starts to go down, performance goes down with it so perhaps a good idea to execute the main priorities in the first half.

> Afternoon, where the dominant element is wind, is when the sun starts to set and it becomes

windy and you feel the afternoon lull. Get some fresh air and move to keep the self awake but begin to slow down.

Evening, where the dominant element is earth, is when the digestive fire is almost out. After having a light dinner, it is a great time to introspect and participate in activities that are grounding.

Night, where the dominant element is ether, is when the body requires rest (suggested time for bed is 10:00 p.m.). Melatonin is heightened between 10:00 p.m. and 02:00 a.m. and is also the time when your body goes into cellular repair mode, which is essential for healing. You may notice that when you fight it and stay awake, your body needs fuel and so you get hungry, giving you a second wind of energy. Ether is dominant between 02:00 a.m. and 06:00 a.m., where after cellular repair, space is created in your nervous system to receive additional information. This is why most find it easier to study or go into a deeper meditation in the mornings.

This methodology allowed my body to work at an optimal level. Are you ready to optimise yours?

EXERCISE

In order to fast successfully, walk before you run. Set yourself a target on how many hours you wish to fast to build up to twenty+ hours so that autophagy can take place. You can start with a fourteen-hour gap. Which is not much longer than between dinner and breakfast and work up from there.

Fasting hours	Date
14 hours	
16 hours	
18 hours	
20 hours	
22 hours	
24 hours	
24 hours+	

With regard to sleep, start becoming aware and note down the times you go to bed as well as the times you wake up. Be aware of how you feel based on the hours you slept, the time you went to bed, and the time and content of your food the night before. You will start to notice a pattern which will highlight your sleeping patterns.

Day of week	Time					
	Dinner completed	Bedtime	Interval between dinner and bedtime	Waking up time	Sleep duration	How do you feel?
Monday						
Tuesday						
Wednesday						
Thursday						
Friday						
Saturday						
Sunday						

All this means that small changes in our diet and sleep patterns can have significant impact on our bodies. Now that you have the tools for decluttering the self, we can transition to external decluttering, starting with people.

7

DECLUTTER PEOPLE

Creating stronger and deeper relationships

Energy is contagious, positive and negative alike. I will forever be mindful of what and who I am allowing into my space.

—Alexe Elle

You already know people in your life who either raise your energy levels or lower them. The question then arises, how do I get more time with those who raise my energy levels and not get affected by those who currently lower them (especially when they are colleagues or members of the family)?

This chapter will enable you to strengthen the relationships you want, regardless of where they are currently. We will be covering different areas pertaining to relationships:

1. Acceptance versus expectations. How to stop your expectations from consuming your time and health, allowing you to break free from the bondage of expectations and reach new heights.
2. Avoiding assumptions. Making sure you are clear about people's intentions, regardless of the method of communication over the voice in your head that may or may not have interpreted it correctly.
3. Overcoming confrontational conversations. Understanding a framework that will give you the best probability of a positive outcome with people who matter.

As you read along, you will be supplied with the tools for creating stronger and deeper relationships as well as removing the bondage of relationships that do not matter.

Do you really know how much strained relationships are affecting you today? I am speaking specifically about the relationships that keep entering your mind on a frequent basis, which are in effect clutter, because they are preventing you from reaching your true potential. Allow me to share two extreme scenarios here:

Someone cuts you off on the road. Being a man of principle, in a situation like this, it would have really ticked me off, and would have resulted in anger, cursing, and, more dangerously, revenge. Imagine, this relationship with someone whom I do not even know, is strained and affecting me to the point where I am out of control. What is worse is that anger is lowering my energy levels and putting me in a negative state of being, lasting for hours, and also damaging my health.

- You refrain from having what you believe to be a confrontational conversation with a loved one. There is so much in the unsaid—whether based on expectations or assumptions—that the mind runs wild. I do not know about you, but my mind would unfortunately think the negative outcome rather than the positive. Over time, I let these thoughts grow, which in turn resulted in either greater distance or friction. Remember, the distance with a one-degree difference in a circle increases over time.

In my case, what prevented me from having these conversations was wearing the mask of making others happy. What is your reason?

THE POWER OF A **ONE DEGREE SHIFT**

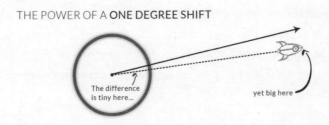

The difference is tiny here...

yet big here

If you're going somewhere and you're off course by just one degree, after one foot, you'll miss your target by 0.2 inches. Trivial, right? But what about as you get farther out?

In a rocket going to the moon, you'd be 4,169 miles off (nearly twice the diameter of the moon). Over time, a mere one-degree error in course makes a huge difference!

The bottom line is, these strained relationships—whether with someone I loved, worked with, or did not know—were affecting me to such an extent that my productivity and health declined. The next section is going to provide tools to overcome this.

In order to create stronger and deeper relationships, and not be affected by the relationships that do not matter, it is important to reflect on the following three areas outlined earlier in this chapter:

1.   Acceptance versus. expectations
2.   Avoiding assumptions
3.   Overcoming confrontational conversations

ACCEPTANCE VERSUS EXPECTATIONS

This is a pretty simple concept. Expectations can lead to disappointment, anger, frustration, etc. It also means that I have not accepted the person for who they are. Let me clear one thing before we continue. I am not referring to expectations which are based on job profile or the universal ones—trust and respect.

Expectations also put undue pressure on others, which essentially harms the relationship. Again, I am not talking about cultural or family expectations that you may have accepted, but rather those expectations that cause a strain as actions are being performed unwillingly. This pushes the person to be someone they are not, and as we already know, it is a lot harder being a second-rate version of someone else over the best version of yourself.

Until a few years ago, Ekta and I had never truly accepted each other wholly. We both wished changes in each other's personalities or bodies. Although small, this caused a rift in our relationship, knowingly or unknowingly. I cannot speak on her behalf, but it certainly made me feel down, especially when it came to my imperfections, such as my chicken legs (I have small calf muscles). If I felt this way, there was no doubt she felt the same way. At that moment I changed my lens and accepted her for everything she is and what she will become. In an instant, the negative bond broke and the positive bond grew in strength, bringing us closer together. This same philosophy was applied to all those around me, and relationships started to blossom, including the relationship with myself.

AVOIDING ASSUMPTIONS

Several years ago, it was highlighted to me that ASSUME stood for making an ASS out of U and ME. This has stuck with me ever since, and through awareness, I think about this every time I make an assumption. In essence, by assuming, I am filling in the blanks with my interpretation of a situation where I do not have all the information, with an unwillingness to ask questions that would have otherwise given me complete information.

Although assumptions could be partially right, it still means they are partially wrong (if not completely incorrect) and can have a damaging outcome, especially when it comes to relationships. Imagine you are acting on an assumption that is based on a reality created in your mind, which most likely will have a negative effect on your family, friends, and colleagues. With globalisation, this becomes an even bigger situation, as behavioural patterns from different cultures vary and what one may consider polite the other may consider offensive.

What are assumptions based on? Usually past experiences and/or things you have heard from others. What makes them worse is if emotion was involved in your past experience and you got hurt. If that pain has not been dealt with, your memory will trigger that pain if in a similar situation, often resulting in an irrational action.

Let me share a story to explain better. Imagine you are running along the beach one sunny weekend morning and a colleague is running towards you. You give a smile and a wave and get nothing in return. This triggers all sorts of negative thoughts and perhaps even some curse words (I will let your imagination run wild). Monday morning in the office, this same individual greets you with a smile and you give a cold reply based on your experience over the weekend. This triggers negative thoughts in them. When you meet at a social gathering later in the week, the two of you don't even acknowledge each other and the friendship is over purely based on assumptions.

So let us go through the facts now. When you were not acknowledged on the running track, you have no clue why. How about reaching out to the individual and checking with them to see if they are OK? If it is unusual for them to behave in this manner, perhaps there is more than meets the eye. The same applies with the Monday morning experience. Because the blanks were filled in with assumptions on both sides, what could have been a fruitful relationship came to an end. Worse still, this also affects your state of being and results in lower productivity as well as other things such as anger, bitterness, etc.

With the world moving more towards text over voice, the danger of assumptions gets even worse. Read the sentence below:

I never said she stole my money.

This seven-word sentence has seven different meanings depending on which word in the sentence you stress. Imagine if the sender meant one meaning and you interpreted another that completely changes the intention of the message. If unclear, reach out!

Think back and reflect on how many relationships have been strained as a result of either side making assumptions. Perhaps this is a good opportunity to reach out. But the conversations in your head may seem confrontational or hard. Let me share how I tackle them in the next section.

OVERCOMING CONFRONTATIONAL CONVERSATIONS

Have you ever felt misunderstood and wished the other person would just take a minute to understand things from your perspective? If we desire this, should it not then only be fair that we provide the same minute towards others as well? Another core value of mine is non-absolutism, the notion that truth and reality are perceived differently from diverse points of view, and that no single point of view is the complete truth. A great example is described below.

A group of blind men heard that a strange animal, called an elephant, had been brought to the town, but none of them was aware of its shape and form. Out of curiosity, they said, "We must inspect and know it by touch, of which we are capable." So, they sought it out, and when they found it, they groped around it. The first person, whose hand landed on the trunk, said, "This being is like a thick snake." For another, one whose hand reached its ear, it seemed like a kind of fan. Another person, whose hand was upon its leg, said, "The elephant is a pillar like a tree trunk." The blind man who placed his hand upon its side said, "The elephant is a wall." Another who felt its tail, described it as a rope. The last one felt its tusk, stating the elephant is that which is hard, smooth, and like a spear.

Do you wish to share your viewpoint but avoid the conversation out of fear? And if you manage to overcome the fear, are you entering the conversation in a negative state of mind such as anger? How would you like to learn about a framework that will allow you to speak freely without regret and maximise your chances of a positive outcome? Below is the framework I follow that has helped me through the years:

1. Approach the conversation with compassion and empathy. If you enter with anger, for example, how do you expect to have a positive outcome?
2. Have clarity on the outcome you are looking for and communicate the same.
3. Outline the protocol below:
   a. No raising of voices and certainly no physical violence.
   b. Do not point fingers but rather talk about how you feel.
   c. No interruptions or distractions; find a quiet place without gadgets.
   d. Listen to the other rather than the voice in your head.
   e. Do not make assumptions; keep asking questions until you have clarity.
   f. Do not judge but rather understand the other's perspective.

Just to elaborate on the listening, I want to stress that I am not talking about passive listening, which is really one-way communication, where the receiver does not communicate back and may or may not have understood the message. I am talking about active listening, which would allow you to accurately reflect what was said, encompassing the feelings or messages that were being conveyed (rather than listening to the voice in your head). This is the basis for trust and respect. A simple example is when I inform you that I will share five three-digit numbers and you can win $1,000,000 if you repeat them back to me—caught your attention, right?

My motto in life has always been to share the truth no matter how hard it may seem. The hardest conversations I have had are with the people that matter most in my life. By following the methodology shared in the previous section, all relationships that matter to me have become stronger and deeper. More importantly, I have been able to remove the clutter in my mind and become freer.

I thought I understood what true love was, until I came across a passage on marriage from Kahlil Gibran's book, *The Prophet*. I would like to share a story about acceptance versus expectations. Prior to Kahlil Gibran entering our lives, it was expected that my wife Ekta and I would do most things together, whether we enjoyed it or not. It almost seemed we were attached at the hip and behaved as one. His passage made us realise that although Ekta and I are husband and wife and love each other very much, we are two beings and it is not necessary for us to do everything together. This was a pivotal moment in our relationship, as it allowed us to be more authentic and accepting of each other. Below is an extract from his work:

Give your hearts, but not into each other's keeping.
For only the hand of life can contain your hearts.
And stand together yet not too near together.
For the pillars of a temple stand apart.
And the oak tree and the cypress grow not in
each other's shadow.

It was the fifteenth wedding anniversary of a very dear friend of mine, and I did not want to be late. I had informed Ekta that we need to leave at 8:00 p.m. in the evening to ensure we reached on time. At 7:50 p.m., it was clear that she would not be ready on time, so I informed her I was ordering a taxi and looked forward to seeing her whenever she arrived. Due to our understanding, I was able to leave in a positive state of mind and she was able to spend the necessary time she required to get ready. It was quite amusing, as several people did not understand why we had not arrived together and it was probable that several assumptions were being made. It did not matter, however, as we had decided to live on our terms and were more than happy with our decision. She arrived within the hour looking as stunning as ever, and we had a wonderful celebratory evening together.

Rewinding to a time before Kahlil Gibran entered our lives, I would have been staring at the clock and making remarks out of anger and frustration because I knew the probability of being late was high. She would feel the time pressure as well as be angered by my constant remarks, resulting in some form of unleashing on me. Basically, we would be angry with one another, sit on opposite sides of the cab on the way to the party, pretend to be a happy couple in front of others, and have a terrible night. You may argue that we ended up spending more on cab fare; however, I would spend that any day to have a sound marriage.

True love can only come from acceptance of the other, converting each imperfection into perfection. I truly, deeply thank Kahlil for his words of wisdom on marriage, which allowed ours to blossom and hope this enables your relationships to soar to new heights.

There are two things that are critical to success when it comes to people: having clarity on the outcome and awareness of your emotions. Without clarity, you are just walking into a forest with no idea about direction. How do you expect to reach a positive outcome when you do not even know what the outcome is?

Be aware of your emotions. Every time you feel you are losing control, you need to pause and regain control through breath work or reflection. Either you need to understand the intentions of the other person, which can be done through questioning, or reflect on the change in your emotional state and understand which triggers are being activated. If you are unaware and you react, which can easily be regretted later, you are essentially the puppet and the other person the puppet master; you are reacting based on what they have said or done rather than being in control. After a pause, however, you are able to reflect and then respond consciously, rather than react.

I can share from experience that I have regretted most decisions I have made when high on emotion. This includes decisions made when high on positive emotions, as I have purchased some expensive items after signing large deals, which turned out to be silly decisions.

Now that you have understood the concept of decluttering people, let me highlight the key takeaways to develop stronger and deeper relationships with those who matter:

1. Have pure relationships. Accept the person for who they are rather than what they are. If there is a problem, speak from the heart with the framework presented to clear the air and create a stronger bond.

2. Everyone is on their own journey. When you begin to remove the physical and mental clutter from your life, the benefits gained will be so great that you will want to push them on your loved ones and colleagues. Even though your intentions may be pure, it will backfire, as they may not be ready. The lesson I learnt is to keep sharing your benefits and allowing them to decide for themselves.

3. Be around people that give you positive vibes. If someone is draining your energy, reflect on which buttons are being pushed through awareness and address them at the core. This way you will either remain natural or gain from positive vibes.

EXERCISE

Before you read further, identify the people with whom you wish to have the talk—the one you have held back for so long—and commit to a date when you will reach out to them. It is time to break down the walls of the past and build for a better future. Pick three and write down a date by which you will call them within the next thirty days.

First Name and Date:
Second Name and Date:
Third Name and Date:

Apart from being an active listener, make a commitment to yourself that you will be more aware and will not let emotions drive you. Remember that reacting in an emotional state without control reduces the chance of success, so take a pause and reply consciously.

Turn the page to read about the final stage of decluttering and finally break free from the shackles holding you down.

8

LESS IS MORE

Declutter material things

Love people. Use things. The opposite never works.

—Matt D'Avella

Imagine a world where you have every material item your heart desires, but there are no people with whom you have a strong relationship to share your joy with. Now imagine a world where everyone has the basic necessities in life, but there are beautiful relationships, joy, and happiness all around.

If you could only pick one, which one would it be?

In this chapter you will understand what you really want and learn about tools to remove the physical clutter that is taking up unnecessary space in your life. I will be covering the following:

1. Having clarity regarding the difference between want and need. We seem to need a lot of things, but are we certain we understand what our needs really are? "I need . . ." is often used; however, in most cases it is a question of desire over necessity.

2. Learning to implement the formula that you can apply to start removing your physical clutter and create space for other things to enter your life.

3. Understanding the benefits decluttering will bring in your life which include, but are not limited to, saving money, saving time, and having more focus on the things that matter more in your life.

People often ask me, what is the difference between decluttering and minimalism? Decluttering is a stepping stone to minimalism where you can start to remove excess after which you can evaluate what you really need and choose to take it a step further towards minimalism, which essentially means owning as few things as possible.

How much of your stuff do you actually use? Imagine how much money you could have saved if you did not buy the things that have not added any value in your life. Imagine the time you could have saved if all those shopping excursions could have been avoided. What passions have you been sacrificing as a result of this behaviour?

I had a reality check when I attended a talk about death, where the speaker highlighted the importance of having discussions with the family around the subject matter and sharing my perspective. It is a conversation that is often the pink elephant in the room. Strange, considering it is the only thing in life that is guaranteed. During this talk, we were asked to write down the five most important things in our life, each on a separate piece of paper. Mine were family, friends, university degree, car, and watch. We were then informed we only had seven days to live and to discard the papers that no longer mattered. I was quick to remove all but family and friends with whom I wanted to share every remaining minute. Why do I need to think about death to want to spend more time with family and friends, building memories that will stay with me throughout my life?

I started to think about my little children—they did not care how expensive or not something was or what brand it was; they only cared if it added joy or function in their life. That was my aha moment, when I realised I had it all wrong. I was lost in brands, gadgets, and luxuries that had started to control me. It is embarrassing to say this, but many of my purchases were also to showcase what I have!

In order to find out who I truly am, I had to declutter from all physical things that in my head were defining me. If something had no functional purpose in my life or did not bring me joy, it was time to break free and take control over myself again.

Before I share how to declutter and its benefits, it is important to understand the difference between "want" and "need." Being a fan of storytelling, let me share a story that highlights this point best.

Towards the end of January 2017, I had the pleasure of summiting the tallest mountain in Africa, Kilimanjaro, with Ekta, Jasmine,

Linda, Maryam, and Zaha. One evening, after our seven days on the mountain, while having dinner, I asked the ladies, "What do you miss the most?" Without hesitation, all of them mentioned their kids. Funnily enough, not one mentioned the husband! As my wife was with me she couldn't miss me, but the question still remains what her answer would have been if I had not been there. ☺ I asked the question again but this time made it clear the answer could not involve people. The three most common replies were:

1. A bed
2. Running water
3. A warm room

When was the last time you were grateful for what I consider the basic necessities of life: food, shelter, and clothing? It was only while living in tents without showers did I value what I otherwise took for granted. This was also the moment I realised that if I could survive with so little on a mountain for seven days, do I really need so much? Most of the things I thought I needed were actually things I wanted and should be classified as desires. It was from that moment onward, I would stop saying "I need" and replace it with "I want." Changing just that one word changed my buying patterns forever.

So now that we know the difference between want and need, let us look at the formula of decluttering from the physical world:

Items you give away (outflow) > new purchases (inflow) = decluttering things

Let me start with how I stopped my inflow. During a retreat I attended at a dude ranch in Idaho in the summer of 2017, I came across an energetic speaker from Australia, Finn Kelly, who shared his experience of not buying anything for a period of one year, and how it changed his perspective on the material world. Although I cannot recall the details of his talk, what did resonate with me was this process of limiting one's "intake." Was I buying too much? Don't I already have enough?

I came back that summer and decided that from September 1 to December 31 of that calendar year I would not purchase anything. The only exceptions were food, gifts for others, and tennis strings in case mine broke (however, if the racquet broke for whatever reason, that was not allowed to be replaced).

I thought I did not shop much, but boy, was I wrong! During the first week, I had to stop myself on several occasions from picking up a magazine or a small item here or there. Bottom line: all the little things add up to a lot! The only way to get through this exercise more easily was to do it through a heightened state of awareness. To elaborate, I would consciously distance myself and observe what was happening in me before taking any action. I would remind myself of this decluttering exercise and ask myself, is this a need, or a want? In pretty much every scenario, it was a want.

What happened over the next few months was very interesting, to say the least. Previously, I would walk by a store and look at the window display and stop when something would catch my attention. I would then evaluate the item—looking at the quality and price—and then determine whether it was affordable and, if it was, when I could look to add it to my collection. Halfway through the "no shopping" exercise, I just stopped looking (with the exception of stunning displays, which were more aesthetic than anything else).

During the exercise, I started making a list of items I would buy from January 1 onwards during the sale (since it made me feel good that I was saving money). What happened during the exercise, however, was that I started crossing items off the list. After giving it more time and asking myself, "Is this a want or a need?" I realised it wasn't really a need at all. Was I buying more on impulse before? While giving this more thought, I concluded that not buying a "want" item was true savings, rather than buying at a discount.

The icing on the cake was that I got to spend more time with my loved ones, and I increased my level of focus since the clutter of materialism was no longer blurring my vision.

Now that the inflow is under control, let us focus on reducing what we have. Everything you own occupies space in your mind rent-free. I am going to use a car as an example to help address this point. Apart from driving the car, you also need to maintain it, wash it, fill it with fuel, get car insurance, renew your registration when required, maintain a valid driver's licence, etc. By selling the car, you no longer have to be concerned about any of the items mentioned and free up a lot of space in your mind. If the item has a functional purpose or brings you joy, go ahead and keep it. If it does not, however, why are you keeping something that is occupying space in your mind rent-free? Would you offer real estate to someone without asking for rent?

Here is the process you can follow to start removing the items that no longer serve any purpose or bring joy, allowing for whatever positivity you want to bring into your life. Start by identifying a room to declutter. Select an area, cupboard, set of drawers, etc. and take everything out, which we will then split into three piles:

1. The first pile represents the items that have a functional purpose or bring joy. These can be put back in an organised fashion.
2. The second pile represents the items that no longer have a functional purpose nor bring joy. Pack these items to give away.
3. The third pile is the "I am not sure" pile. This could include items that no longer have functional purpose but have a memory attached to it or used to have functional purpose (for example, clothing that no longer fits).

Let me share some insights about the third pile to make it easier for you:

1. Although the items no longer have a functional purpose in your life, it will offer functional purpose in someone else's life. In my case, I gave a lot of my items away to those who are less fortunate than me, so essentially, I was decluttering for smiles.
2. The process cleared up space in my house.
3. By giving the item away or selling it, the memory still remained and did not leave with it.
4. In the case of clothing that did not fit anymore, keep it if it inspires you to get back to that size but remove it if all it does is put you in a negative space. Why on earth would you want to do that?
5. If all the above do not apply to you, put the third pile in a box. If the box is unopened for several months, say three to six months, clearly you can do without those things.

Remember, this exercise is not in place to make you anxious, so only do what you feel is comfortable. In my case, at the time of writing this book, I had gone through a decluttering process of my cupboard four times in a span of three years, each time filling more than a suitcase. I am sure there will be many rounds to come, as I realise what is really essential in my life.

Who would have thought that an exercise as simple as decluttering things could add so many benefits to my life? To make your life simpler, I have highlighted the five benefits below:

1. I realised that I actually need very little.
2. I have more free time to spend on my passions, as I am spending much less time when it comes to shopping.
3. I am saving money through fewer purchases and making money from selling certain items I no longer need.
4. I have greater focus on the things that matter the the most, as I am not thinking about what I need to buy, which I now see as a distraction.
5. I am making a difference in the lives of those less fortunate than me, which has a great feel-good factor to it.

I would like to share with you two stories that highlight additional benefits gained as a result of decluttering from material things.

START GOOD HABITS BEFORE THE KIDS BECOME ADULTS

Prior to my journey into decluttering, we used to go through the kids' stuff and remove items that were no longer appropriate, getting a little of their input when it came to toys. I realised that kids are natural at decluttering (as they grow out of stuff) and we should involve them in the process. At least once a year, we now declutter our home as a family and explain the benefits to the children, including the concept of decluttering for smiles. I have seen them evolve and become a lot more giving than before, and now they only keep things that have functional purposes and bring joy.

In December 2019, we spent one week volunteering in a school for the underprivileged in the small town of Palitana in India. Pretty much all luxuries of the life we were used to were stripped away, yet this happened to be one of the best holidays we had ever had. The time we spent with each other and the lovely people we met was truly a testament to the value of relationships and the little joys in life. These school children, who had so little, had smiles from ear to ear and such big hearts. One girl who had become fond of our daughter gave her one of her coloured pencils she'd got on her birthday. This brought tears to my eyes, because she had so little and yet she was so giving. She wanted to spread joy rather than keep it all to herself by opening her heart.

We now focus a lot more on experiences over material gifts. The children rarely ask for things and value the memories we build together. I have to be honest; it is not only the kids who have benefited but Ekta and I too, as our interest in materialism has greatly reduced. In fact, for my fortieth birthday, I received only experiences as gifts from friends and family with the exception of one book titled Walden, which was about simple living in natural surroundings. ☺

REUSE AND REDUCE WASTE—LOVE FOR MOTHER EARTH

After climbing four mountains, spending days in the Amazon rainforest, a trip to Bhutan, and numerous trips to the mountains for skiing, one thing that is clear is Mother Earth is beautiful. The more time I spend in nature, the more I realise that we need to shift to a mindset of reuse and reduce over buy and throw/recycle. We are now a lot more conscious of what we buy and happy to accept hand-me-downs from others. When you see such natural beauty in its purest form with minimal intervention from mankind, you want to make sure you preserve it to enjoy in your lifetime and preserve it for the next generation.

For this to work, you need to keep asking yourself why you buy the things you do and be honest with yourself. Is it to showcase to others (why would you need to spend over $10,000 on a watch when your phone gives you the time), ask yourself what is it that you want to prove? Does this highlight some other insecurity?

Perhaps you buy something because it makes you feel good, but many a time, you may have reflected and realised that the purchase was a mistake. If it is the feeling that you are after, think of other activities where you get the same sensation and focus more on those rather than impulse buying.

Lastly, spend more time with those who have less than you and quickly you will realise that you are blessed with more than what you need.

I never really understood the meaning of less is more until I started on this journey of decluttering.

Less stuff = more space
Less stuff = more money
Less stuff = more time
Less stuff = more focus

Now that we are clear on the difference between want and need, let us start replacing "I need" with "I want." It is amazing how the mind shifts when we switch from thinking something is a necessity to understanding it is a desire.

You also have the formula to declutter things, which is to ensure that you are buying less than you are giving away. When you do desire to buy something, hold on to that thought and ask yourself if you want it. If the desire is as strong three days later, then go ahead and buy it; however, you will notice that the desire has reduced, if not disappeared, within that timeframe.

Less stuff = more freedom

The biggest benefit gained from decluttering the material world is breaking the bond between you and physical items. Detachment does not mean you do not own anything. It means nothing owns you. You simply own the item for the comfort it is providing in your life—nothing more, nothing less.

Now it is time to take action and start the decluttering process. As you will see below and in the rest of this book, the key is momentum. Once you start to see and, most importantly, feel the benefits, you will find the energy to declutter all areas of your life. For the best chance of success, answer these questions below:

1. For how long will you stop all purchases as described in this chapter?
2. On which day over the next seven days will you start decluttering?

3. Which room will you declutter first?
4. How many items do you commit to giving away?

If you really want to be bold, announce it to the world. Once you make it official, you will feel more accountable.

You are so close to breaking free from the physical world. There is one more area to be covered, which is digital decluttering, to regain control of your life.

BONUS CHAPTER: DIGITAL DECLUTTER

Be the master, not the slave

Technology is just a tool.

—Melinda Gates

You may have been wondering why I have not yet covered the rise of technology. Before I continue, I want to highlight that I am a tech geek. That is primarily why I chose to pursue bachelor's and master's degrees in electrical and electronics engineering—purely because of my passion for electronic gadgets.

The real question you have to ask yourself is, "Do you control the technology or does the technology control you?"

To help you answer, let me ask you a clarifying question—in general, do you stop what you are doing when the phone rings to answer it OR when you get a notification? If you answered "Yes" then your technology controls you.

With the advancement of the smartphone giving us the ability to work, play, share, learn, communicate, and stave off boredom, we now use these mobile gadgets more than ever. So, the follow-on question is, are you addicted to your smartphone? Below are some signs and symptoms according to the *Entrepreneur* (https://www.entrepreneur.com/article/273682):

1. Reaching for the phone first thing in the morning.
2. Using your phone when bored.
3. Increasing phone use.
4. Becoming anxious or agitated when the phone is out of sight.
5. People complaining about your phone usage.
6. Inability to cut back on your phone usage.

Still confused? Ask yourself if you can disconnect for twenty-four hours? If your answer is "No," you are addicted.

Although many of my stories from the mountain will be shared in my next book, where I talk about scaling your summit in more depth, I will share one reflection. Every time I scale a mountain, I usually have limited or no connectivity with the rest of the world. What the mountain taught me is that things are still going to move forward, whether I am connected or not. When this became apparent, I started to question my habits around technology and reflect upon how they were affecting both my sanity and productivity.

Once I was clear—I was an addict—I had to remove the clutter. I implemented a nine-step strategy:

1. I switched off all notifications, whether it was a pop-up, sound, or vibration.
2. I only answered calls during times when I was able.
3. I started to charge my phone outside the bedroom and would not check it for the first two/three hours of the day.
4. I deleted all apps that no longer served any function.
5. I started to check emails three times a day and set up an autoresponder highlighting this.
6. I unsubscribed from all unwanted newsletters.
7. I stopped watching TV with the exceptions of documentaries and a movie here or there, as I was addicted to shows and my mind would be diverted to entertainment over my life goals.
8. My phone would not be visible during meals and the TV would be off.
9. I stopped following everything and everyone on social media that was no longer in line with my life's goals.

In essence, I took control of my life again and technology became my slave.

Now we have broken the bondage to the physical world. Congratulations on completing the four-step decluttering process. This is not going to be easy, and you will encounter many hurdles in your journey. Turn the page to learn how you can overcome them to finally liberate yourself.

9

BREAK FREE

Remove the clutter and go deeper within

They did not know it was impossible, so they did it.

—Unknown

Are you aware of your self-limiting beliefs? How many times have you stopped your progress because you decided it was not possible? Why are you holding back from the greatness you are capable of?

Are you ready to remove your self-limiting beliefs and move forward and break free?

You have worked so hard to get to this stage and understand the tools required to remove the physical and mental clutter from your life. Even though you understand the benefits, are you finding it hard to make changes because your mind is conflicted?

In this chapter I will share the steps I took to overcome each hurdle:

1. Removing self-limiting beliefs. How many times have you been the greatest obstacle to your progress? How many times have you come close to breaking free only to go back to your comfort zone? I will share techniques that helped me reduce my obstacles.
2. Which voice do I listen to? Your mind is saying left and your heart is saying right, putting you in a spot where you are conflicted. I will share which one I pick and why.
3. Finding your purpose. How great would it feel knowing why you were born? The good news is that there is no need to be anxious about it, as I will reveal the answer.

Have you ever felt like you are running but you are not clear about the direction of your life? Do you wish there were more hours in the day to complete all your tasks and priorities? Is this causing greater levels of stress and anxiety?

That was me.

When I turned forty, I started to ask myself a lot of questions including, what is my purpose and where do I see myself at the age of seventy? Although I had a lot of short-term goals for myself, the family, and the business, I was completely blank about the life I wanted.

Then it hit me. If I do not know where I am going, why am I running in turbo mode in several directions? I felt like the ball in a pinball machine going in all directions whereas in reality I wanted to have clarity about my summit. It was time to take a step back and start preparing a list of things I did and did not want out of life. I will share what came immediately to mind.

What I did not want: I did not want to wake up one day and look back at life and feel regret. Regret that I did not do what I should have done. Regret that I did not spend enough time with my loved ones. Regret that my health had deteriorated to the point where it put stress on the rest of the family. I knew that once I had clarity on my end goal, it would make all my decisions easier as I would only say yes to those that were in line with where I wanted to go.

What I did want: I wanted to spend more than half my time giving back to the world in the field of education. Although my purpose was not clear at this point, I felt that every child being educated would resolve several of the problems we face in the world.

This process allowed me to have clarity on purpose and know the life I wanted to live, which went into detail such as my daily schedule. Now that I had clarity on what the summit was, it was time to scale it.

How can you know your summit? Let me share my three-pronged approach below.

REMOVING SELF-LIMITING BELIEFS

It is time to take control of your mind, to replace "I can't" with "I can and I will." How do you even know you cannot when you have not even tried? Not trying means you failed before even attempting it. How do you expect to succeed with that mindset?

On the morning of May 6, 1954, Sir Roger Bannister ran the first sub-four-minute mile (three minutes and 59.4 seconds, to be precise) breaking a record held for nine years. Up to that point, people believed it was impossible to run a mile in less than four minutes. Once he showed the world it was possible, the record he set was broken in just forty-six days by John Landy, who ran the distance in three minutes and fifty-eight seconds. It is astonishing that a record that took nine years to break was broken in just forty-six days! You may ask, how did this happen? The mindset changed from "it is impossible" to "it is possible."

Think of your mind like the fuel tank in a car. Even when my car would highlight the total distance remaining, based on the level of fuel, as 0 km, I was still able to drive several kilometres to the nearest fuel station. The car manufacturer has put this in place to protect us and ensure that we get fuel in time to avoid our car stopping in the middle of the road. This is the same as our mind, which in reality is working to protect you from pain and suffering, as it knows your fears, insecurities, and lies. The question you have to ask yourself is, how much further can you go? How much reserve do you actually have that is yet untapped?

In December 2006, Ekta and I started our journey to Kala Patthar, a black rock situated a little higher than the base camp of Mount Everest, at an elevation of 5,645m (18,520ft). This had been a dream trip of mine for years, and I was blessed that Ekta decided to join me along with one of my closest friends, Ramsey, on our first mountaineering experience. After trekking for nine days, as we stopped for lunch, the weather was not looking too good to continue to Kala Patthar; hence, we started to wind down mentally. As it happens at high altitudes, the weather completely changed while we were eating and our lead guide mentioned that there was a window of opportunity to keep going and have the chance to see the sun set on Mount Everest.

Although we were tired, we did not want to lose this opportunity and started the ascent. The final stage was mentally and physically challenging: we were physically tired but still had to climb over the large rocks in the final stretch; the air was thin, and it was becoming harder to breathe with our oxygen levels reducing (oxygen levels are 50% of sea level concentration). It was challenging enough that one of the two guides had to stop and go down as he was getting symptoms of altitude sickness. All of a sudden Ekta broke down and said she could not go on, even though we could see the destination in sight. She had great difficulty breathing and felt that someone was suffocating her. If she took one more step, she felt she would collapse. Physically and mentally she was depleted but pushed me to go on, as this was my dream she was supporting and did not want to be the reason for me to miss out, especially when we were so close. I turned to her and told her that whatever we do, we would do it together, be it going up or down. We had already succeeded in getting this far and going down would not be considered a failure.

This story still brings tears to my eyes, as what happened next highlights the strength of the mind when you tap into the reserves. I do not know if she did it for herself or for me or both, but she found the strength to continue hand-in-hand with me until we reached Kala Patthar and watched Mount Everest and the surrounding mountains turn gold as the sun set on the Himalayas, one of the most magical memories I have ... one that we both would have missed if she had not tapped into her reserves and found the strength to carry on.

WHICH VOICE DO I LISTEN TO?

Every now and again, you come to a junction where your mind tells you to go in one direction and your gut, heart, or soul (there are many descriptions used for this; however, I will use soul) tells you to go the other way. Which voice do you listen to?

In my experience, I have found that the best decisions are made when the soul and mind are in balance. If there is too much weight on either side, the outcomes do not turn out in my favor. The challenge occurs when I am in balance but must choose one direction. Being an engineer by education, my belief was always in logic, and hence I would allow my mind to win even if it may have felt wrong.

With the entry of spirituality in my life, I now always go with soul over mind. How did this shift happen? My personal belief is that the soul that is housed in my body during my lifetime is connected to the divine and has infinite knowledge. The mind, which is part of my body has limited knowledge, which is based on my learning and life experiences. So when I have to decide between limited knowledge and infinite knowledge, the choice becomes easy. The question then becomes, how can I be sure I am listening to my soul? It could be emotion or even the mind.

This is where the practice of meditation and silence has helped me to see with more clarity by removing the clutter and going deep within to connect with the divine. During my daily meditation, I am able to slow my mind down from sixth gear to first gear and listen to my soul. The most inward I have gone was during my silence retreat in February 2020 (Vipassana), where I stopped communication entirely. For those who are not aware, that means no phones, computers, TV, talking, communication, or connection of any kind. The purpose of this was to be able to go deeper within and find the answers you are looking for. The experience was so magical that I have decided to practise this every year for the next six years. Although I could write another book on my experience and learning, my key learning from this retreat was **only the truth**. I know this sounds simple but reflect on how many lies, no matter how big or small, you may say daily? I had decided to be truthful to myself and to all around me, no matter the consequences as truth always prevails.

Here is the thing: my inner voice has always been there but I chose to suppress it. Now I take the necessary measures, be it meditation or time alone, to listen to it loud and clear, especially when making big decisions.

FINDING YOUR PURPOSE

> *The two most important days in your life are the day you are born and the day you find out why.*

—Mark Twain

This whole thing of knowing my "why" was actually causing me a lot of stress and anxiety, especially since it was so clear for Ekta. Now I do not mean this with any negativity such as jealousy, but when Ekta had clarity and I did not, it just added to the level of anxiety. If anything, she was very supportive of the whole ordeal.

This is when I realised that this was actually becoming clutter in my life, as it was holding me down in several areas of my life and so I stopped thinking about it.

Here is the good news: there is a universal purpose for all of us and that is for our soul to depart our body in a better state than it entered. In a nutshell, just be a good human being to yourself and those around you as well as your communities.

Why is this purpose thing important anyway? Purpose provides a meaning in your life and gives you a sense of place. Once you have found purpose, it is easier to know where you belong. In addition, people with purpose live longer and live healthier lives than those just running on autopilot day in and day out.

In my case, while reading a book on the way of life, the light bulb in my mind suddenly went on and all became clear to me. My purpose in life is non-violence (ahimsa). This includes non-violence to the self and to all other living beings including animals and Mother Earth. Now that I think back, here are the signs that may help you to define your purpose with more clarity:

1. When you donated time, money, or talent to helping others (or even thought about it), what were the areas and why? In my case, it was always environment and education of children (my belief was education would eradicate many global problems).

2. Who are the people you are attracted to? I have always been attracted to people who are making a positive impact in the world.

3. What are people saying about you? Reach out to people and ask what reminds them of you. See what you hear and see the commonalities that form.

4. What are the injustices that bother you? What makes you so unhappy that it bothers you to the core?

5. Discover what you love to do. What do you truly love that you can do all day, every day?

Consider what type of skills, talents, and passions you bring to the table. Then, brainstorm how you might turn your passion into something meaningful to you. Imagine living each day doing something you are passionate about and good at and which the world needs, and getting paid for it. This is a concept that the Japanese refer to as *ikigai*.

Based on a book by Hector Garcia and Francesc Miralles, ikigai is a Japanese concept that means "a reason for being." The word refers to having a direction or purpose in life, that which makes one's life worthwhile, and towards which an individual takes spontaneous and willing actions, giving them satisfaction and a sense of meaning to life.

At the time of writing this book in May 2020, I spent a good portion of my day living out my purpose of ahimsa. Seems like a dream come true. Without removing my self-limiting beliefs, listening to my inner voice, and living with purpose, however, I would not be here today. That does not mean I would never have gotten here, but I am glad I figured it out as I turned forty; otherwise I would be living a good life rather than an awesome life until much later.

How did it all begin, you may ask. In June 2018, as I was standing at the bar of the closing event held by the Entrepreneurs' Organization, James Samuel came over and informed me that knowing about my journey had a profound effect on his life and that I should not keep it to myself. I should share it with the world. On the drive home that night, I shared the conversation with Ekta and told her perhaps this was a sign, as that is what my inner voice was telling me. This is the same voice I would have ignored in the past, but after concluding the link to the divine, I took it a lot more seriously.

That same summer, while going through my morning routine in my in-laws' house, my inner voice told me to stop and go to the library. I went down the stairs into the library and started reading my book. Once again, the inner voice told me to stop and scan the library. Although all the books were standing so that you could only see the spine, one book was staring at me, *Jain Way of Life*. The aha moment came to me when I saw the image below:

Earlier that year in February, I was blessed to have a spiritual leader, Brahmrishi Guruvanand Ji Maharaj, share his wisdom with our dear friends at our home. Upon completing his discourse, he gave me a locket with the image above and his blessings. At that time, however, I had no idea what this symbol meant.

The description under the symbol in the book read "ahimsa," which means non-violence. It was as if someone had handed me the final piece of the puzzle and the image became clear. My purpose was to spread ahimsa in the world. It almost felt like I knew it all along but never really reflected upon it. Now it was crystal clear.

When I returned to Dubai, the local Entrepreneurs' Organization chapter was experimenting with a new "in dialogue" series where they wanted to hear about the journey of a member. This was my opportunity to share with others through a trusted platform, and so I reached out to Ruchir Punjabi, one of the learning chairs at the time, to explore whether my topic of decluttering would fit their requirements. Having seen part of my journey, Ruchir was quick to add me to the series with my first talk being scheduled in February 2019. Although the two talks within Entrepreneurs' Organization turned out to be very successful, they were dialogues—which is more two-way rather than a presentation, which is one-way. I then reached out to Aparna Verma, the owner of Clarion school, who opened up her heart and school for what would be my first public appearance. With a little marketing, I had over thirty people attending and got rave reviews from several of the attendees. Although the feedback was overall positive on all fronts, and my inner voice and purpose were aligned, I was still not convinced that I was good enough (my self-limiting belief) to present to the world because everything until now had been without any income.

It all changed when I received a call from Rakhee Kantaria from Nairobi, who had heard about my talk and wanted to invite me for a paid speaking gig for the Kenya chapter of the Entrepreneurs' Organization. The local chapter of YPO (Young Presidents' Organization) heard I was coming and signed me up too.

Now that my self-limiting belief was removed, it was time to do what I was born to do and live each day with passion and purpose.

In order for this to work, you will have to be very clear about direction. If there is any doubt, the changes in your life will look and feel like sacrifices, whereas if you have clarity, they will simply feel essential.

Michael Singer outlined it best in his book, *The Untethered Soul*, where he basically said you think you are free but in reality, you are holding yourself back. He continues by telling you to imagine yourself as a dog with a shock collar around your neck. You do not see it, but there is an electric fence (one that you cannot see) around you and every time you get close to it, you feel the pain from the shock collar. You see freedom on the other side, but you choose to go back to your comfort zone.

How many electric fences do you have around you? What is stopping you from running right through and enduring a little pain in order to become free? What are you afraid of? It's not who you are that holds you back but rather who you think you are. Nothing is more painful than being stuck where you do not belong. Time is limited. Don't waste it living someone else's life. Have the courage to follow your heart and intuition. The pain of regret far outweighs the pain of risk.

Every time I ran through the fence and endured pain, I asked myself if I had made the right decision because it affected my relationship with Ekta. We were no longer able to share food and desserts, as I had become vegan. I would no longer buy anything for her that was damaging Mother Earth and was non-essential such as flowers and jewellery. I would rarely socialise on weekdays as I had to be in bed by 10:00 p.m. I stopped watching TV (with the exception of documentaries and movies) and rarely went to the cinema and replaced it with spending quality time with loved ones. Each decision hurt our relationship temporarily and she became more distant because she could no longer relate to who I had become. I would hear comments such as "I don't even recognise you anymore" or "You are not the person I married," to which I replied, "This is the real me, 100% authentic." I knew if I stuck with my inner voice and purpose, I had nothing to fear. I had worked too hard to get to this stage, which was to feel amazing. I could not go back to how I used to feel. Through a commitment towards one another and constant communication, we learnt to accept each other for who we are and our relationship became stronger than it has ever been.

Freedom is important because it leads to enhanced expressions of creativity and original thought, increased productivity, and an overall high quality of life. Freedom is to live without fear.

From this chapter, you have learnt that living with purpose allows you to live a more meaningful life, and now you are aware of the universal purpose that is relevant to all living beings. This gives you the strength to make the necessary changes to avoid waking up one day and looking back on your life with regret.

If you really want to know whether you are fulfilled or not, ask yourself what you would do if you had only thirty days to live. The question becomes, why are you not doing those things now? Is it the self-limiting beliefs that are holding you back? No problem, you now have the tools to tap into your reserve and start achieving that you had deemed impossible. Is it the conflict between your soul and your mind? No problem, you now have the tools to go deeper within through meditation or aloneness to find all the answers within.

Are you ready to do what is required to become liberated?

Here are some great tools to implement to liberate yourself:

1. Make a list of self-limiting beliefs and reflect on their origins as well as how you can overcome them.
2. Make a list of everything you would do if you only had thirty days to live. Write down when you will do them so you do not live with regret.
3. Start spending more time in aloneness through meditation or silence so you can go deeper within without the clutter of your daily life and listen to your inner voice. How about one day to disconnect completely with everything and everyone?

Be patient and take your time. You are about to make major pivots in your life to live with passion and purpose.

The four-step decluttering process brought us to this chapter, where you learnt to liberate yourself to achieve greatness and be the rock star that you are. Turn the page to review the conclusion of this book and start paving the path to a liberated version of yourself.

FINAL CHAPTER

Congratulations on completing this book and taking the necessary steps to remove the physical and mental clutter in your life and breaking free to get peace within. Breaking free is essentially detachment but what does that even mean? Detachment does not mean you do not own anything. It means nothing owns you, giving you the freedom you are looking for. A great example of this is the smartphone to which many people have given a lot of power, being hooked on it all day and taking it everywhere they go (I admit, I was guilty of this). While being lost in the smartphone, you are essentially missing out on all the beauty around you in the world. It's time to establish a relationship in which you are the one in control.

You may have come across the saying "Yesterday is history, tomorrow is a mystery, but today is a gift. That is why it's called the present." Here is the thing though; you are unable to enjoy the present to its fullest as you are carrying the clutter of the past and future everywhere you go.

Break free from the weight holding you down, allowing you to become lighter and liberate yourself. See what has already been achieved through implementing the insights from this book and imagine the possibilities that are yet to come as you continue this journey.

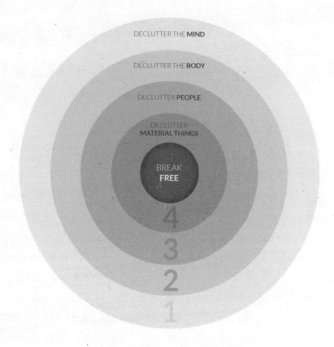

In order to succeed, I am going to request that you pick one or two items at a time to declutter to increase the probability of success and ideally to start with decluttering the areas that are in your control (usually the outer layers of the circle). As you break free and start to see and feel the benefits, this will provide the momentum to keep going and you will benefit from the following:

1. More time to pursue your passion and priorities.
2. Greater focus and awareness in all areas of life.
3. Stronger and deeper relationships with those who matter.
4. Starting each day high on energy and clear on purpose.
5. Living your life with love and joy rather than fear and stress.

Most importantly, you will have the tools to break free and feel liberated.

Below are the most common objections I have heard from people before commencing on this journey:

I am too busy and simply do not have the time.

Breaking free will allow for greater clarity, making your day more efficient by clearing up hours and allowing you to have more time than you do today.

It sounds too hard/I do not have the discipline.

You have to ask yourself how badly you want it. If you are just interested, there will be small changes. If, however you are passionate, there will be transformation. When your purpose and belief system are clear, there is no sacrifice but only clarity, focus, and eagerness.

I enjoy some of my clutter and do not wish to give it up.

It is about adding things that are more in line with the direction you wish to take, allowing decision-making to become much easier.

Once you focus on areas that matter more, the things that are less significant will slowly fizzle away.

I would like to plant a seed before we move to the next section. Are you spending so much time to earn money and power that you are sacrificing all other areas of your life? Is money something you are constantly chasing? Whatever money you are chasing, let us just assume you have it. Now that you are rich, reflect on the areas of your life you are unhappy with. These are the areas you should be working on now rather than when it is too late.

Decluttering is not a destination but rather a journey in which you are going back to your pure state, which is of love and compassion. You are going back to live a life full of purpose and achieve greatness, because you are a beautiful soul, always have been and always will be. Shout it out for the world to hear, "Freedom, here I come!"

I have always dreamed of being a rock star. The problem, however, is that my voice will repel the audience rather than attract them. Here is the thing—I am a rock star. I just didn't know it was for spreading non-violence in the world. Remove the clutter in your life and be the rock star you were always meant to be.

The mission of this book is to provide you with the tools to break free from the weight holding you down, to overcome mental overload, and scale your summit to live a healthy, stress-free life with financial abundance.

I am truly humbled that you chose to invest your valuable time to learn from my journey. Should you have any questions as you embark on your journey to break free or wish to accelerate your progress through a more customised approach, feel free to get in touch on saahil@saahilmehta.com

I cannot wait to hear about the positive changes that you have made in your life as a result of breaking free from the physical and mental clutter in your life. Please feel free to reach out to me directly if you have any questions or require further assistance.

Now that you have all the tools to break free, as soon as you put the book down, take the first step today. This book was not only to inspire but also to transform, and we certainly do not want procrastination to get in the way. Let me share a story about a sailor.

The sailor went to the captain to get his wages and was told to come tomorrow. The next day, he gets up all excited and goes once again to the captain only to get told, "Didn't I tell you tomorrow?"

So, you see my friend, tomorrow never comes. Act today and take the first step to live the life you were always meant to live.

I would like to take this moment to commend you for accessing your leader within, your inner authority that leads by example, standing in full self-acceptance and claiming full self-authority of your life's journey. The leader within has always been a part of you. By removing the clutter and breaking free, the divine light has spread to all parts of your body to give you what we all yearn for . . . freedom.

EXERCISE

Just when you thought you were done, I am going to give you one final exercise, which will allow you to see how much you have progressed since the start of your journey.

Complete the wheel of life and give yourself a ranking out of ten for each section once more. How much have you improved? How much further do you wish to improve? Continue to identify the clutter and break free.

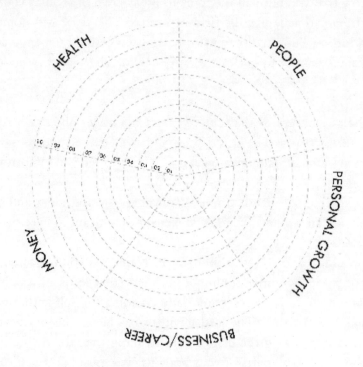

While my story ends here for now, yours is about to begin. And I invite you to begin your journey of breaking free by decluttering from all the four dimensions of your life with me.

I have created an exclusive community of folks who are committed to breaking free from their illusions and self-imposed limitations. Join this group of amazing leaders from all walks of life, from all across the world, who are inspiring and enriching each other in this journey of personal transcendence.

We have created an accountability tribe on our private Facebook group: "Break Free with Saahil Mehta," where I continue this conversation and you continue your momentum.

Once a week we will get together to help you stay true to your commitment of growing into the best possible version of yourself, as we together learn to build new rituals that help us scale our personal summits of happiness and success faster than ever before. Plus there will be a lot of exclusive content that I will be sharing with you regularly to help you stay accountable to yourself and stay truly committed on this journey, because what I have learnt over the last four years is:

Change is made easier with the right tools.

Transformation is made pleasant with the right attitude.

Growth is made possible with the right mentors.

The transcendence you experience when you commit and continue this journey is glorious, euphoric, and simply worth it.

Scan this QR Code and join our BREAK FREE tribe today.